HISTORIC SCOTLA

SCOTTISH ABBEYS AND PRIORIES

HISTORIC SCOTLAND

SCOTTISH ABBEYS AND PRIORIES

RICHARD FAWCETT

B. T. Batsford Ltd/Historic Scotland

For Tim and Clare

First published 1994

Typeset by Goodfellow & Egan Ltd, Cambridge
and printed in Great Britain by
The Bath Press, Bath

Published by B T Batsford Ltd
4 Fitzhardinge Street, London W1H 0AH

A CIP catalogue record for this book is available from
the British Library

ISBN 0 7134 7440 8 (cased)
       0 7134 7372 X (limp)

Contents

Illustrations

Colour plates

Acknowledgements

In writing this book I have had help from many people. In particular it is a great pleasure to thank Professor Geoffrey Barrow, Dr David Breeze, Dr Mark Dilworth and Mr Christopher Tabraham, all of whom read through the draft text and offered me much helpful advice and assistance. Despite their help, however, I must accept responsibility for the views offered here. I also owe thanks to Mr Martin Wilson, who remodelled the plans to my requirements.

Unless otherwise stated in the captions, all photographs are copyright Historic Scotland.

Introduction

With a few notable exceptions, of which Iona and the Border Abbeys are perhaps the most obvious, the monastic remains of medieval Scotland are not widely known. This is unfortunate, because Scotland played a distinguished role in the history of monasticism and, considering its relatively limited resources, it invested a quite disproportionate part of its wealth in building abbeys, priories and friaries. It should not be forgotten, for example, that Iona's contribution to the Christianization of Britain in the seventh century was more permanent than that of the better-known Kentish mission of St Augustine. It is also the case that the future David I was the first patron to introduce one of the reformed monastic orders to Britain in the early twelfth century, with the foundation of his Tironensian house at Selkirk. One further point worthy of note is that at least two of the orders which found fertile soil here, the Tironensians and the Valliscaulians, were either barely or not at all represented in England. This shows that Scotland was by no means dependent on her southern neighbour for guidance, but was in direct contact with the main centres of monastic life.

There are probably two main reasons why Scottish monasteries are not well known. One is that neither the monastic churches nor the conventual buildings attached to them have survived particularly well; the other is that not enough has yet been done to make available information about what does survive. On the first point, monastic churches were not well-suited to the forms of worship which developed in Scotland after the Reformation of 1560, in which preaching came to be the main element. Although many had long served as both parochial and monastic churches, and thus tended to continue at least partly in parochial use for a while, the majority progressively fell out of use. On the second point, Scotland did not have the benefit of an upsurge of scholarly interest in her medieval church architecture from the earlier nineteenth century onwards, as happened in some other parts of Europe. Much of the basic groundwork for understanding it therefore still remains to be carried out, though in recent years renewed activity has been encouraged by the great strides made in the study of the history of the medieval church as an institution. There has also been a recent increase in the more scholarly archaeological investigation of sites, and we now appreciate that there is great scope for expanding our understanding of monastic sites by such means.

This book, however, is intended as a survey of the surviving buildings of the Scottish religious orders. It was felt it would be most useful for the general reader – at whom it is aimed – if it offered initially a chronological account of the surviving remains of their churches, set against the background of the

circumstances within which they were produced and the religious life they housed. This
is then followed by a separate treatment of
the planning of the monastic buildings.
Finally, in appendices at the end, there are
brief accounts of the various orders that
found a place in Scotland, followed by a
gazetteer describing the main sites. By
arranging the book in this way it is hoped it
will be possible to help readers understand
the buildings that were the physical expression of the monastic life more clearly, and to
appreciate the spiritual foundation that
underlay the construction of some of the
most inspiring buildings ever raised on
Scottish soil.

CHAPTER ONE

The Earliest Monasteries

This book is mainly concerned with the architectural remains of the houses of monks, canons and friars of medieval Scotland, and with what they can tell us about the lives of those for whom they were built. Because so little survives above ground of our earliest monasteries, the book concentrates on the buildings that were produced between the great period of the reorganization of the church in the earlier twelfth century and the Reformation in 1560. However, Scottish monasticism has a much longer history than that, going back at least to the mid-sixth century and, since we can only understand later developments if we have some appreciation of those earlier phases, we must spend a little time considering them – despite there being so little to see on the ground. But before that it may also be helpful briefly to consider the origins of Christian monasticism itself.

The origins of monasticism

In a faith which places such a high emphasis on inner spirituality as does Christianity, it was inevitable almost from the beginning that some of the more devout souls should wish to turn away from the temptations and distractions of the world in order to devote themselves more completely to God. This was especially the case after Christianity had become more institutionalized as a result of

the official standing granted to it in the late Roman empire by Constantine (306–37). The earliest recluses were hermits or anchorites, large numbers of whom were enduring lives of isolated self-imposed deprivation in the deserts of Egypt, Syria and Palestine from around the late third century onwards. One of the best known of these hermits was St Antony, who withdrew into the Egyptian desert in about 270. For many, however, and particularly for those who could not aspire to such singleness of purpose, the religious life was better followed with the moral support provided by fellow ascetics. For them life in the organized community of a monastery was a safer path to fulfilment, and ultimately to salvation. One of the first monasteries was that founded by St Pachomius, also in Egypt, in about 320. Such communities might embrace a wide range of human types, from the simple to the intellectual, and could include both the aristocrat and the peasant. It is also important to appreciate that most members of early monasteries were not ordained priests.

The ideals of monasticism, emphasizing stability and obedience, were gradually more completely formulated through the writings and activities of a number of great leaders. These included St Basil the Great, who became bishop of Caesarea in 370, and John Cassian, who had experienced monasticism in the Holy Land and went on to found monasteries in Gaul in about 410. But the greatest father of monasticism in the west was St Benedict of Nursia, who established the monastery of Monte Cassino in southern Italy at some date after about 525 (**1**). He soon afterwards compiled a rule for his monks which has been the main basis of the monastic life in western Christendom ever since. This rule was to some extent a compilation from the writings of a number of earlier monastic leaders, though the way in which the pursuit of high spiritual attainment was tempered both by the recognition of human frailty and by sheer common sense marks Benedict as a leader of special genius.

Iona and the arrival of monasticism in Scotland

We do not know when Christianity first reached the areas that were eventually to become Scotland, but it is likely to have been in the sub-Roman period. When St Ninian returned to Scotland in the early fifth century, for example, it was evidently to minister to a population that was already at least partly Christian. Even more difficult to establish is the date when monasticism reached Scotland. But here it is perhaps advisable to remind ourselves of the variety of the peoples who occupied Scotland around this period, since historical circumstances meant that Christianity reached some sooner than others.

In the south of the country, below the Forth–Clyde line, the inhabitants were basically of the same British stock as was found down the western side of England and into Wales, though from the seventh century those Britons in the south-eastern parts of Scotland were increasingly dominated by the Angles of adjacent Northumbria, and Anglian domination eventually also spread to the south-west. The native population north of the Forth–Clyde line was made up of the various tribes that had come to be known by

1 *St Benedict as the father of monasticism (by permission, British Library, Arundel 155 f.133r.).*

the Romans as the Picts. The western Highlands and Islands, however, had been occupied by the Scots who originated in neighbouring Ireland, and the area was known by them as Dalriada.

This picture changed considerably over the centuries, with the Angles, for example, pressing northwards and westwards until prevented from further northward expansion in the late seventh century. Even more significant were interlinked developments in the ninth century when, on the one hand, the Scots extended their rule eastwards over much of Pictland and, on the other, the Norse and Viking raids started the process which was to lead to their occupation of the Northern and Western Isles together with parts of the northern and western mainland.

At the time of Ninian's mission to the Britons of Whithorn, it is likely that only the Britons and the Irish had significant numbers of Christians among their population, and in our present state of understanding it seems more likely that monasticism reached mainland Scotland through the latter rather than the former. In this connection it must be remembered that the main form of church organization in the late Roman empire consisted of a system of territorial divisions known as dioceses, each of which was ruled by a bishop. These dioceses were initially based largely on the administrative divisions of the empire, with the bishops having their principal church in the chief city of each. St Ninian was probably a bishop. Such a system proved to be unsuited to conditions in Ireland, however, and by the sixth century the natural centres of church administration there were monasteries founded by the dynasties which ruled the various parts of the country. There were bishops in Ireland, of course, to carry out the functions for which they were indispensable, such as the ordination of priests and the consecration of other bishops; but in general they had less effective authority than the abbots of the great monasteries, each of whom was usually drawn from the same dynasty as the local king. It was monasticism of this sort that in the 560s was introduced to Scotland at Iona, which is the earliest Scottish monastery about which we know anything with reasonable certainty.

Although the Christians of Ireland considered themselves as faithful sons of the universal church, with the pope as their head, their remoteness from Rome meant that a number of differences of observance had tended to develop, of which a different means of calculating Easter was to become one of the most controversial. The form of the monastic life was also rather different from what was emerging in mainland Europe, being less communally organized and in some ways rather closer in spirit to that of the earlier monasteries of Egypt. Each monk spent much of the day in his own cell, practising extremes of ascetic self-denial, with long periods spent in contemplation, prayer and fasting, as well as physical labour. The founder of Iona was St Columba, or Colum Cille ('Dove of the Church'), a member of the Northern Ui Neill dynasty, who was born in County Donegal in about 521. He established the abbey, on its island off the southern tip of Mull, in either 563 or 565. All of the companions who came with him, and most of his immediate successors as abbot, were also members of his own kinship group.

The spread of Columban monasticism

The Irish church, unlike that of the Britons, placed great emphasis on missionary activity, and at least three important monasteries in Burgundy, for example, along with houses in Switzerland and Italy, had their origins in a mission which set out from Ireland under the leadership of St Columbanus in about 590. Columba himself was to make several excursions through northern Pictland, eventually gaining favour at the court of King Bridei, near Inverness. But conversion must have been a slow process, and the Venerable Bede's claim that he converted the northern Picts is an exaggeration. Nevertheless, there is evidence of a number of monasteries being founded under the influence of Iona both before and after Columba's death in 597. Among those founded during his lifetime were houses on Tiree at Artchain and MacLuinge, that in the Garvellochs at Eileach-an-Naoimh, together with houses at Hinba on Jura, at Cella Diuni on Loch Awe, and others on Eigg and Lismore. Somewhat later monasteries appear to have taken shape at Abernethy, Applecross and Kingarth, and perhaps also at Whithorn, the seat of Ninian's diocese. Very little is known of the buildings that served any of these.

The single most important foundation to be made from Iona took place in 635, although the seeds of Iona's own eclipse were sown in the process. In 633 Oswald, the son of King Ethelfrith of Northumbria, made a triumphant return from exile in the west of Scotland, where he had been converted to Christianity on Iona. Having successfully reclaimed the throne of Northumbria, in 635 he invited Aidan, a monk of Iona, to establish a monastery on the island of Lindisfarne, as a base from which to convert his kingdom. From there prodigies of missionary activity were carried out, as part of which a number of monasteries were also founded in those parts of southern Scotland that were under Northumbrian control. These included Old Melrose, Abercorn and Hoddom, where there may earlier have been bishops' churches, and Tyninghame; Whithorn also eventually became a Northumbrian monastery.

However, the differences between Irish and Roman observances were a growing cause of friction and, in the time of Oswald's brother and successor, Oswiu, there was some embarrassment at the occasion of his second marriage when two separate Easters had to be celebrated because of the different ways of calculating its date. Eventually a synod was called at Whitby in 663-4, at which it was agreed that Roman practices should be followed. A period of some confusion followed within Scotland. Adomnan, Columba's biographer, who had succeeded to the abbacy of Iona in 679, was persuaded to accept the Roman system in 688, but failed to carry his monks with him. The problem was made more difficult by political circumstances, and in particular by a phase of aggressive Northumbrian northward expansion in the later seventh century; this was only halted by the defeat at Nechtansmere in 685 of the Northumbrians under Ecgfrith by the Picts led by Brudei. Nevertheless, despite the Pictish victory, only twenty-five years later their king, Nechtan, sought advice from

Abbot Ceolfrith of Monkwearmouth in Northumbria on how he could bring the church in his lands into conformity with Roman practices. By about 716 even the monks of Iona had bowed to the inevitable, and the golden age of Columban monasticism as a distinct manifestation was at an end, though Iona itself was to show remarkable powers of survival against overwhelming odds.

The planning of the early monasteries

From the limited information available, it seems there could be considerable variety in the way that early monasteries were laid out. So far as we can understand Iona itself in the time of Columba, its limits were defined by a rampart, or *vallum monasterii*, which both set the monastery apart from the world and provided some measure of defence. Parts of this are still visible, though it is clearly not all of one period, since some parts are of single and others of double construction (2). Within the roughly rectangular area enclosed by the vallum was an irregular spread of buildings, the form and layout of which is likely to have been changed relatively frequently since they were of impermanent construction and could be easily replaced. Adomnan, in his life of Columba, said these buildings included a church with an attached chamber, a hut where Columba slept and another where he wrote, huts where the monks worked and slept, guest houses, and structures which served the communal uses of refectory and kitchen. Many of these were built of wattle, though oak was brought from the mainland for at least one of the communal buildings.

Excavation has found traces of several such structures, though it is unclear how far they may date from the time of Columba himself. The earliest substantial stone structure is the building known as 'St Columba's shrine' at the north-west corner of the later church. Because of the way its side walls extend slightly forward to form pilasters (known as *antae*) to each side of the main front it clearly predates the buildings of the Benedictine abbey, but such a building seems unlikely to have been erected before the ninth or tenth centuries. By that stage Iona had produced even more impressive evidence for its artistic creativity in the three magnificent eighth- or ninth-century crosses traditionally said to be dedicated to St John, St Martin and St Matthew (3).

Few of the religious settlements founded as part of the spread of Columban monasticism can have been of any great size. Where there are physical remains it is often the vallum enclosing the main enclosure that is the main feature. At Deerness in Orkney the rampart

cutting off the promontory site may partly date from this period, although a case has been made that it survives from an Iron Age fort, and this could also be true elsewhere. There are remains of what appear to have been settlements of hermits on a number of precipitous promontory sites, as at Sgòr Nam Ban-Naomha on Canna. Two phases of drystone constructed buildings have been identified there, around which extends an oval enclosure wall nearly 2m (6½ft) thick. At Annait on Skye a rectangular oratory and about three circular cells occupy a ridge between two rivers, with a vallum and ditch across the approach to the site. A number of related complexes in the Northern Isles have also been convincingly identified as eremitic monasteries, such as Kame of Isbister in Shetland. One site which has remarkably complete remains is at Eileach-an Naoimh in the Garvellachs – although its completeness is partly due to recent restoration (4 and

2 The remains of part of the earthwork vallum around the early monastery at Iona.

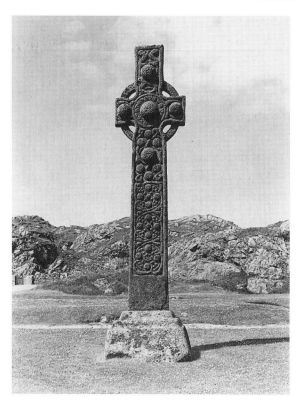

3 St Martin's Cross at Iona, with the rocks of Torr an Abba behind.

4 (Right, above) *The cells at Eileach-an-Naoimh. The construction of these stone-roofed cells, with the masonry laid as inward-stepping horizontal courses rather than as true vaults with radially-set stones, has suggested they could belong to an early religious settlement. This is possible, although such structural techniques remained in use over a long period.*

5 (Right, below) *This group of stones at St Andrews was carved in the years around 800, and probably formed part of a sarcophagus in one of the early churches of Kinrimund. The royal themes, including King David with the lion and a hunting scene, could suggest it contained the body of one of the kings of that period.*

colour plate 1). The corbelled roof construction of the conjoined circular cells can be compared with examples on Skellig Michael in Ireland, and the tradition that they belong to a community founded by St Brendan the Navigator, who died in 575, may not be entirely unacceptable. Of a rather later date may be the hermit's cell on the remote island of North Rona, to which a living cell was subsequently added, and there is a similar two-part arrangement on Luchubran, the Pigmies' Isle, which is rather closer to the Butt of Lewis.

Of the monasteries founded from Iona's Northumbrian offspring, there are tantalizing remains at Old Melrose, where traces of a vallum cutting off the promontory in the meanderings of the Tweed are still visible. More significant remains of the eighth and ninth centuries have been found through excavation at Whithorn, where two conjoined timber buildings on the same axis may have formed a church. Ancillary buildings associated with the monastic foundation at Hoddom, in Dumfriesshire, have also been found. Not long after these structures at Whithorn and Hoddom were completed, however, it is likely that the first waves of Viking attacks were already beginning to have their impact on Scottish monasticism.

Monasticism in the ninth, tenth and eleventh centuries

Orkney underwent a Norse attack in 794, and both Orkney and the Western Isles suffered in the following year. With the further raids of 798 down the west coast, many of the smaller monasteries in that area received a death blow, while the next waves of attacks on Iona in 802 and 806 made it necessary to withdraw the greater part of the community even from there in 807. Eventually, in 849, the treasured relics of St Columba were divided between Kells in Ireland and Dunkeld at the heart of mainland Scotland. The latter, which may have been the site

of a Columban monastery, now became the administrative centre of the Scottish church. This marked an eastward shift of the centre of gravity of the Scottish church around the time that the rulers of the newly united kingdoms of the Scots and Picts were also moving eastwards.

Only a little later, following an attack on Dunkeld itself in the 850s, the centre of the Scottish church was moved yet again, to the east coast site of Kinrimund, eventually to become known as St Andrews (5). From this period onwards, however, until the turn of the eleventh and twelfth centuries, our knowledge of Scottish monasticism is very slight. Some monastic centres do seem to have enjoyed great prestige for a while, and it is hard to imagine that Constantine II, king of the Scots, would have abdicated to become a monk at Kinrimund in 943 if it had not been a place of high standing. Certainly the outstanding artistic quality of the stone sculpture produced at that site since about 800 says much for both its continuing vitality and wide contacts.

Perhaps the greatest innovation at this period was the introduction of a type of religious life from Ireland represented by the Culdees or Celi De (servants of God). In origin the Culdees had been some form of monastic elite, though in Scotland the term was soon being applied to various of groups of clergy. In some cases they do indeed seem to have been groups of individuals living a hermit-like existence, as may have been the case at Inchaffray in Perthshire. In other cases, however, they were evidently groups of secular clergy serving the bishops' churches, which, from around the tenth century, appear once again to have been becoming the main centres of church government. By the start of the twelfth century there were apparently at least two bodies of clergy at Kinrimund, for example, one of which was referred to as consisting of Culdees, although both groups could have been married and may have held their office hereditarily.

In fact, there is evidence that by as early as the tenth century Scottish monasticism was generally no longer in a healthy state, other than in a very small number of centres, of which Iona was again one. Many of the higher monastic offices were regarded as little more than hereditary perquisites for the great families – a situation that was to re-emerge in a different form in the sixteenth century. At Dunkeld, for example, we know that two abbots were killed in battle in 965 and 1045; but these were almost certainly lay officers who had little to do with the spiritual life of the communities they nominally headed. Certainly, the abbot who was killed in 1045 was married to a daughter of Malcolm II, and the son of the marriage was to succeed to the throne as Duncan I, who is best remembered for having been killed by Macbeth in 1040. Even a son of Malcolm III and St Margaret could be both earl of Fife and abbot of Dunkeld. By that stage, however, monasticism within Europe was in the throes of a tremendous period of renewal, in the course of which its great figures were becoming the moral and spiritual leaders of the church. The time was also ripe for change in Scotland.

CHAPTER TWO

The Monastic Revival of the Early Twelfth Century

St Margaret and the later eleventh century

The turn of the eleventh and twelfth centuries witnessed a remarkable revival of monasticism throughout Europe, in which Scotland was eventually to become closely involved. The first stages in this process can be dated to the years following the marriage of Malcolm III to St Margaret in about 1070. Margaret was a princess of the Anglo-Saxon royal house. She had spent much of her childhood in Hungary, where her family had taken refuge in the time of the Danish kings, and when she was again forced to seek sanctuary after the Norman conquest she found it in Scotland. Margaret was an intensely pious woman, and she must have been rather disturbed by the state of the Scottish church at that time. Nevertheless, she was tactful enough to extend her patronage to some existing communities, including Iona, and she also encouraged pilgrimages to St Andrews through her support of the Queen's Ferry across the Firth of Forth.

Other established communities also prospered during her time, though we have no idea if she took any direct interest in them herself. Those at Brechin and Abernethy (6) were able to start handsome Irish-inspired round towers at a period which is likely to have been either before, or not long after, her death in 1093. The former, which rises to a height of 26.5m (87ft) below its later spire, has a particularly finely carved doorway (7). The latter tower incorporates earlier work at its base, but the Romanesque form of its belfry windows suggests it was not completed before the early decades of the twelfth century. Its doorway has a strip-work band around it, and is similar to the doorway at the base of the square tower of Restenneth,

6 *The round tower at Abernethy.*

7 *The carved doorway of the round tower at Brechin. It has a crucifixion at its apex, unidentified saints on the jambs and crouching beasts flanking the threshold.*

one of the most controversial problems in Scottish architectural history and, on balance, it must be said that its architectural details are probably more at home in the early twelfth rather than the later eleventh century. More will be said about this below.

A similar plan was also used for the church that housed St Margaret's most important contribution to the Scottish church, the small community she founded at Dunfermline, where there was an established royal residence. She and Malcolm had been married there, and she built a church to commemorate this, which was served by what was almost certainly the first cell in Scotland to follow the rule of St Benedict. To establish the core of the community she wrote to Lanfranc, the newly-appointed archbishop of

which is also likely to date from the later eleventh century (8).

Although much rebuilt in the twelfth and thirteenth centuries, the tower at Restenneth possibly originated as a small square porticus, with a slightly wider part to its east. A related plan is also to be found underlying the original core of the church known as St Rule's at St Andrews, and it has been suggested that this was the one church said to have still been in use at St Andrews by the earlier twelfth century, and that it therefore must have been built towards the end of the previous century. But the date of St Rule's is

8 *The south doorway of the tower at Restenneth.*

Canterbury, who was spearheading the modernization of the English church for William the Conqueror, and from him obtained three monks. Excavations in 1916 showed that the earliest church at Dunfermline had a rectangular chancel and a small square nave; the latter was presumably surmounted by a tower since its walls were thicker.

Dunfermline seems to have been the only representative of mainstream European Benedictine monasticism to be founded in Scotland in the time of Malcolm III and St Margaret. However, there was an attempt to found another in about 1075, on the site of the earlier community at Old Melrose, but this was to have been dependent on Durham and, since its leaders refused to accept the authority of Malcolm III, they were expelled. Ironically, one of those leaders was Turgot, who later became prior of Durham, and was to be St Margaret's spiritual adviser and later her devoted biographer.

The tentative first steps towards reforming the church and introducing modern monasticism that had been made in the time of St Margaret were almost certainly wiped out in the reigns of Donald Ban and Duncan II in the 1090s. It was only in the reigns of three sons of Malcolm III and Margaret that a new momentum for reform was built up. The first of those sons, Edgar, may have established the groundwork for the Benedictine priory of Coldingham in Berwickshire when he granted the lands to Durham, and he was certainly present when a church was dedicated in about 1100. Beneath the later choir and crossing, excavations in 1854 revealed the foundations of an unusually elongated choir ending in a semicircular apse, and they were possibly part of the church dedicated around 1100. Edgar also obtained a fresh infusion of monks from St Anselm of Canterbury for Dunfermline in the early twelfth century. He may, in addition, have enlarged his mother's church there, since the excavations of 1916 revealed traces of an extension to the first building consisting of a larger choir, wrapped around the end of the earlier choir, and ending in an eastern apse.

King Alexander and the Augustinians

By this stage, however, the urge for a revival of purer and stricter forms of cloistered life was encouraging the emergence of new orders in the more religiously active parts of Europe. Most of these new orders were of monks who were returning to the original spirit of the rule of St Benedict. However, other forms of religious life were also taking shape, and among these were groups of clergy who were not monks but who wished to have their lives directed along a similarly disciplined path as that of the monks. Because they lived according to a rule these communities were known as regular canons (the Latin word for rule is *regula*). Many of them were also known as Augustinian canons because they considered they were following the teachings of St Augustine of Hippo, who had died in 430.

Under two archbishops of York important communities of Augustinians were founded in northern England, including one at Nostell in Yorkshire, and these were in turn to have considerable influence in Scotland. Alexander I, the second of the sons of Malcolm III and Margaret to succeed them on the throne, was supportive of the Augustinians. He founded a priory at Scone soon after 1120, bringing its first canons from Nostell. He also planned houses for the order at St Andrews, Inchcolm and Loch Tay, though the last of these may never have been founded, and the other two only reached fruition in the reign of his younger brother David I.

St Andrews was a particularly significant foundation, because it was also the church of Scotland's leading bishop. After a difficult period, shortly before his death in 1124 Alexander appointed as its bishop Robert, the prior of his new foundation at Scone. Alexander's intention was that the most important church of his kingdom should be served by clergy organized on up-to-date lines. Robert, as an Augustinian himself, naturally wished to replace the existing clergy by a properly constituted chapter of Augustinian canons, though by this stage it was more usual outside the British Isles to have chapters of non-monastic clergy at a cathedral. It was, however, to be some years before Alexander's and Robert's ambitions could be achieved at St Andrews.

The work of David I for the Scottish church

If much of what his parents and elder brothers did for Scottish monasticism has a rather tentative air, by contrast David I set about reorganizing the church within his kingdom with a gusto which is almost breath-taking. As complementary elements in this process he gave a new impetus to the establishment of bishops' dioceses, and encouraged the formation of parishes, by means of which there was a two-tiered network of churches serving the spiritual needs of the whole kingdom. But, most important for our present interests, he was extraordinarily open-handed towards the religious orders. In doing all of this he was certainly appreciating that a well-organized church would be a powerful tool in establishing centralized control over his unruly kingdom. But this suggestion does not discount the importance of his own deep piety; without that he would not have alienated so disproportionate a part of the royal patrimony to the church that James I commented ruefully in the early fifteenth century that his saintly predecessor had been 'a sair sanct for the croun'.

David was the sixth and youngest of his parents' sons, and his prospects of succeeding to the throne must have seemed remote. He was therefore sent off to England, to the court of his brother-in-law, Henry I, where he was eventually married to the richest heiress then available, Maud Countess of Northampton and Huntingdon. As an English – as well as a Scottish – magnate he acquired a close knowledge of developments within the church both in England and on the Continent. He showed a particularly keen concern for the house of Cluniac monks at Reading, which had been founded by his wife's first husband, and whom he therefore succeeded as patron. The Cluniac order had developed from the monastery established at Cluny in Burgundy in 909, and was a major contributor to the modernization of the church in the eleventh and twelfth centuries. But David also became an eager benefactor of other English and Welsh houses of a variety of orders.

It seems he was particularly interested in the newer and stricter orders that were emerging around this time, including the Tironensian and Cistercian monks, and the Arrouaisian and Premonstratensian canons. Following the admission to the order of St Bernard of Clairvaux in 1112, the Cistercian order had begun the extraordinary period of growth which was to make it by far the most influential in Europe. The fact that almost unmanageably vast numbers of new recruits were attracted is particularly remarkable, since the extreme privations the monks imposed upon themselves reduced their life expectancy. The Tironensians represented a similar attempt to return to the spirit of the rule of St Benedict, and David founded a house for them at Selkirk as early as about 1113. It is a clear indication of his important place in the history of monastic patronage that this must have been the earliest house for any of the newer orders to be founded anywhere in Britain. He was evidently so keen to find out more about them that he went to visit their founder, St Bernard of Tiron. The saint unfortunately died before his arrival, but David did at least bring back with him from Tiron a further colony of monks. The Arrouaisians and Premonstratensians represented parallel attempts to introduce a rigorous discipline to the life of the canons.

It is uncertain how many monasteries David founded in Scotland both before and after his succession to the throne in 1124 because, although several houses established during his reign were founded by his magnates, we cannot be sure how far David himself was involved in a number of such cases. Nevertheless, the following list will give some idea of his personal involvement.

For the Benedictines he re-established his mother's priory at Dunfermline as a major abbey in 1128, and he also played a part in the foundation of priories on the Isle of May, at Rhynd (Perthshire) and at Urquhart (Moray). For the Tironensians he founded Selkirk in about 1113, which was moved to Kelso in 1128, and he joined with Bishop John of Glasgow in founding a priory at Lesmahagow in 1144. He introduced the Cistercians to Scotland at Melrose in about 1136, and founded Kinloss in 1150; he almost certainly also contributed to the foundation of the Cistercian houses at Newbattle in about 1140 and at Dundrennan in 1142.

So far as the orders of canons are concerned, he founded major houses for the Augustinians at Holyrood in 1128, and at Jedburgh (again, along with Bishop John of Glasgow) in about 1138. He possibly also founded smaller houses at the ancient sites of Loch Leven and Restenneth in about 1150 and 1153 respectively. At these the adaptability of the canons made them obvious candidates to introduce on sites where there was a wish to supplant an existing community of Culdees or other clergy. Also for the Augustinians he completed his brother Alexander's foundation of Inchcolm at some time before his death in 1153, and was similarly involved at St Andrews. For the Arrouaisians he founded Cambuskenneth, in the shadow of Stirling Castle, in about 1140,

though this was later absorbed into the Augustinian order. He may also have played some part in founding the Premonstratensian abbey of Dryburgh in about 1150, even if the main responsibility there was that of his Constable, Hugh de Moreville.

In addition, he almost certainly founded the houses of Knights Templars at Temple and of the Knights Hospitallers at Torphichen. Beyond all of this, he may have been involved in founding a Cistercian nunnery at Berwick-upon-Tweed.

Taking account of all of the other endowments he made to the church, and allowing for the relative poverty of his kingdom, this was beneficence on a prodigious scale. Many of the churches and nearly all of the monastic buildings raised for the abbeys and priories founded by him have been destroyed. But there are significant remains of the churches at Dunfermline, Kelso, Holyrood, Inchcolm, Jedburgh, Loch Leven, Restenneth and St Andrews, while the plan of the original church at Melrose is at least partly known through excavations.

The smaller monastic churches built for David I

There is a remarkable variety in the monastic churches built for David I, from the magnificence of the royal mausoleum at Dunfermline Church, to the diminutive fragment at Loch Leven. The architecture of these churches also reminds us that David had first-hand experience of the buildings being produced over a wide area, and drew masons from several of those areas in response to a scale of architectural demand which Scotland was technically quite unable to meet at this time.

Loch Leven probably started as a simple church with one rectangular compartment for the nave and a smaller one for the chancel to its east, rather like the earlier churches built at Dunfermline and Restenneth. A third compartment, possibly a tower, may have been later added to the west, entered through an archway in the west wall, though it is no longer possible to be certain about this. Despite its small size and very simple detail, a fine feature of this church is the quality of its masonry, which is of large rectangular blocks of finely-jointed stone. Masonry of this type was to be characteristic of several of the churches built for David I, including the church of St Rule at St Andrews, and the upper stages of the tower added to the priory church at Restenneth. The latter has rather curious triangular-headed belfry windows, which have been thought to point to an earlier date for the tower, though parallels which may be of the twelfth century can be found for them at Dunfermline.

A larger version of the type of church seen at Loch Leven survives as the earliest part of the church on another island site, at Inchcolm. The church on Inchcolm was augmented on several occasions in the thirteenth century by the addition of a tower, a longer choir and a single transept, before being replaced by a completely new church further east in the fifteenth century. But it is still possible to see the remains of at least one round-headed window, and of the doorway in the west wall. The arch of the latter was carried on nook-shafts – free-standing shafts set into an angle of masonry – and had capitals of the type known as cushions, with a flat semi-circular shape on each face; perhaps the archway in the west wall of Loch Leven also started as a similar doorway.

The finest and most complete of this group of churches, though, is St Rule's at St Andrews (9). As has already been said, this church started its life with a two-part plan – a tower-nave and a chancel – which is likely to date from after the time that Bishop Robert was eventually consecrated in 1127. The rather old-fashioned details of the earliest work at St Rule's, like those in the tower of Restenneth, have suggested to some writers

that it dates from the late eleventh century, and this cannot be completely ruled out. In particular, the horseshoe-shaped arch between the nave and chancel, and the way in which the chancel windows have their internal arches cut from single blocks of stone and their external arches cut into the horizontally-coursed masonry, have been thought to point to an early date. However, bearing in mind the difficulties that there must have been in finding sufficient masons to carry out the great new wave of church building that was taking place around this time, it is hardly surprising that not all of the imported masons were in the vanguard of architectural innovation.

Not long after the first part of the church of St Rule's was built, it was extended by the addition of a nave to the west of the tower, and by what was perhaps a presbytery to the east of the chancel. It may well have been Bishop Robert's eventual success in overcoming the resistance of the existing bodies of clergy, and establishing a community of Augustinian Canons in 1144, that was the reason for this enlargement. To give access to these new additions arches were cut through the west wall of the tower and the east wall of the chancel, the details of which are similar to those of the tower at the small church of Wharram-le-Street in Yorkshire. The significance of this similarity is that Wharram was a church which belonged to Nostell Priory, where Bishop Robert had earlier been a canon; and so it seems likely that, in extending his church, Robert had sought masons from his old home, colleagues of whom were also at work at Wharram. It was through such connections that craftsmen

9 The tower and original chancel of St Rule's Church at St Andrews. The arch in the east wall is a later insertion made at the time the church was extended eastwards.

were found for the new spate of work in Scotland, as is evident also in some of the more ambitious building operations.

A building which served as a link between the smaller and the greater churches built under the patronage of David I is that of the Augustinians at Holyrood. In 1911 excavations revealed that the first church there had a simple rectangular choir and an equally simple rectangular nave. But it was given a more complex plan by the provision of transepts – cross arms – between the two parts, each of those transepts having a square chapel on its eastern side for additional altars. The only part of this church to survive above ground is a doorway at the east end of the south nave wall, which gave access from the church to the monastic buildings around the cloister on that side (10). This doorway offers a link between the architectural detailing of Inchcolm and what we shall find at Dunfermline, and reminds us that even a relatively small church could be handsomely decorated.

The greater churches built for David I

The three churches which now best illustrate David I's highest architectural aspirations for Scottish monasticism are those at Dunfermline, Kelso and Jedburgh, which were built respectively for the Benedictine, Tironensian and Augustinian orders. The architectural range demonstrated by the three is quite remarkably varied. The first was the burial place of David's parents and of a number of his brothers, and was destined to be David's own last resting place. Family piety and dynastic pride therefore dictated that it had to be a building of great scale. For Kelso and Jedburgh a major reason for their size was that they were on the border with England, and national honour demanded that David demonstrate to England that his abbeys were the equal of theirs. But at Jedburgh there may have been an additional reason in that Bishop John of Glasgow, the co-founder, had recently returned to his diocese after a particularly bruising tussle with the pope and the archbishop of York over who was in charge of the Scottish church. (It should perhaps be mentioned here that, while Kelso was in the diocese of St Andrews, Jedburgh was within that of Glasgow.)

Only the nave of the church which David started at Dunfermline in about 1128 survives. However, from records made before a new church was built on the site of the choir in 1818–21 we know that the eastern limb was originally three bays long and had an aisle down each flank; at the east end was a semicircular apse as the setting of the high

10 The south nave doorway at Holyrood Abbey. The capitals of the nook-shafts are of scalloped design, and the semicircular arch has two orders of characteristic chevron (zigzag) decoration.

11 *A reconstruction sketch of Dunfermline Abbey church, showing it as it was probably first planned (Harry Bland).*

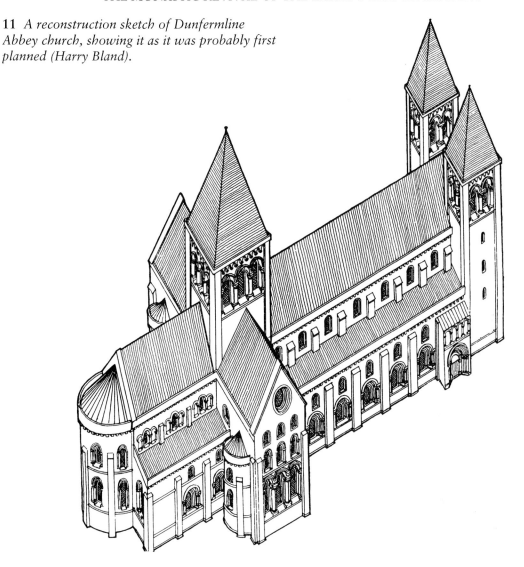

altar (**11**). There was an aisled nave of eight bays with a pair of towers over the western bays of the aisles, and marking the distinction between the eastern limb and the nave were transepts, with a central tower over the crossing. In this arrangement the ceremonial area around the high altar, known as the presbytery, was at the far east end of the building. The choir of the monks would have stretched westwards from it, and may even have extended into the eastern part of the nave. The nave of the abbey church served the local people as their parish church, and their main altar would have been against the western side of the stone screens which closed off the monks' choir. There would also eventually have been other altars in the aisles (**12**).

On the basis of the architectural parallels, David must have brought a number of masons from Durham Cathedral to design and build Dunfermline, and it was perhaps fortunate for him that a pause in the building operations there had recently resulted from the death of Bishop Flambard. The first building phase probably embraced the whole of the eastern limb – since that part would be needed as soon as possible – and the lower

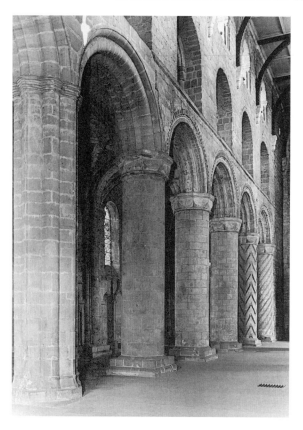

12 The nave of Dunfermline Abbey church. The decorated piers at the far end may have marked the site of the main nave altar; the octofoil pier at the west end is part of the mid-fifteenth-century rebuilding in this area.

parts of the nave. Although Dunfermline was only about half the size of Durham and did not have stone vaults over the high central spaces, with all the extra support that required, in these earlier parts of the work the similarities between the two buildings are seen in many details. These include the decorative arcading below the large round-headed windows in the aisles, and the incised spiralling and chevron decoration of the great cylindrical piers at the east end of the nave, which probably marked the siting of the main altar in the nave. In the decorative arcading of the aisle walls Dunfermline was less complex than Durham, where two levels of arches intersect with each other; while in

the pier design the absence of high vaulting at Dunfermline resulted in a simple sequence of cylindrical piers rather than Durham's alternation of cylindrical and more massively constructed piers. Nevertheless, allowing for the differences of scale, the similarities between the two buildings are striking.

Even more specific links with Durham are seen in the capitals of the splendidly carved doorway which opened from the church into the cloister around which the domestic buildings of the monks were ranged (13). This is the most ambitious of the three twelfth-century doorways, and is fortunately particularly well-preserved because it was covered by a burial enclosure for about three centuries after the Reformation. The carvings of the great west doorway are more restrained (14).

By the time the upper parts of the nave of Dunfermline were being built, however, it looks as if the Durham masons had left. In common with most major churches at this time, the main spaces of Dunfermline were three stages high. Above the two rows of arches known as the arcades, which opened into the aisles on each side, were arches opening into galleries between the vaults and the roofs over the aisles; above all of that was the stage known as the clearstorey, with high windows set behind a mural passage. At Dunfermline the galleries and clearstorey were very plain by comparison with the arcades and aisles, and it could be that masons trained at a much less ambitious building than Durham – such as Carlisle perhaps – had been brought in around the middle years of the century.

The abbey church of Kelso, which was re-sited from Selkirk in the same year that Dunfermline was started, is a more puzzling building, particularly since so little of it remains (15). However, we do know that, instead of being laid out on the cross-shaped plan usual for major churches, it was planned as a double cross, with a transept at the western end as well as between the choir

13 *The capitals on the western side of the southeast doorway opening from Dunfermline Abbey church into the cloister. The rich foliage designs of these capitals are closely related to examples in manuscript painting, and remind us that such stonework was originally painted. Nevertheless, the basic cushion or scalloped forms that were common in capitals at this period are still suggested in the underlying forms of the design.*

and nave. Such a layout had been adopted for several churches in the German empire from around the early eleventh century, and a number of major churches were built to related plans in eastern England in the late eleventh and early twelfth century, as at Ely and Bury St Edmunds. But the architecture of Kelso is like none of those, and it is very difficult to know from precisely where the idea was drawn.

14 *The capitals on the southern side of the western doorway, Dunfermline Abbey. These illustrate the three basic types of Romanesque capital design: the cushion, with a single semicircular curve to each face; scallops, with two or more curves to each face; volutes, with an overhanging curved form at each angle that is ultimately copied from the Corinthian capitals of classical antiquity.*

15 *Kelso Abbey church in the mid-nineteenth century. The surviving part of the three-storeyed nave is to the left, the western tower at the centre, and the north-western transept to the right (W.H. Lizars).*

Excavations in the 1970s suggested that the nave was six bays long between the two sets of transepts and, while the western set projected very little beyond the aisles, the main transepts were probably of quite wide projection. The grand entrance to the church was in a western porch which rose the full three-storeyed height of the central space of the nave, and there was a shallow porch for the lay folk who used the nave in the north face of the northern transept. Only two bays of the main body of the nave survive, on its south side. They show that the arcade was relatively squat; above that the middle storey is a wall passage, with a continuous sequence of small arches opening towards the central space, while the clearstorey had a similar sequence of small arches. However, a surprising feature is that the rhythm of arches at all three levels is completely independent. By this date it was usual for the division into bays indicated by the piers of the arcade to be continued up through the upper storeys; but there was nothing of this at Kelso. This may have been partly because the upper storeys towards the west end of the nave were only completed towards the end of the twelfth century, and certainly their architectural details are later than those of the arcade. But it seems likely that this unusual arrangement extended down the full length of the nave, and was intended from the start.

An important source of information on Kelso is a description preserved in the Vatican archives, which dates from 1517, among other things, it provides the following information:

> The monastery ... is ... conventual ... but it also has an extensive parish; ... at each end it has two projecting chapels ... which give the church the likeness of a double cross .... The entire roof of the church is wooden. It has two towers ... crowned by pyramidal roofs .... The church is divided by a transverse wall into two parts; the outer part is open to all, especially parishioners, both women and men, who there hear masses and receive all sacraments from their parochial vicar. The other part ... takes only monks who chant and celebrate the divine office .... The high altar is at the head of the choir .... There are besides, in the whole church, twelve or thirteen altars on which several masses are said daily, both by monks and secular chaplains. In the middle of the church, on that wall which divides the monks from the parishioners, there is a platform of wood; here stands the great crucifix .... On the same platform there is also an organ of tin.

This description brings out admirably not only the specific peculiarities of planning of Kelso, but also reminds us of the clear physical division that there was between those parts of an abbey church which were reserved for the monks, and those parts which might be used by layfolk.

Moving on to Jedburgh, we find yet another approach to design, and an even more forceful reminder of the range of architecture with which David I must have been familiar. If the masons who designed Dunfermline were drawn from northern England, and the design of Kelso possibly shows the influence of ideas developed earlier in Germany and eastern England, for Jedburgh it is likely that masons were brought from southern or south-western England. Of the church started around 1138, only the western bays of the eastern limb and parts of the transepts

survive, but excavations have suggested that it had a rectangular aisle-less presbytery; this was followed by two aisled bays and then by transepts which each had a semicircular apsidal chapel on their eastern side. Such a plan showed some similarities with the church that had been started at Southwell in Nottinghamshire a little earlier in the century, although at Southwell the aisles also had apses. This is also a reminder that the designers of new buildings very seldom took their ideas from just one other predecessor; instead, patrons and their masons are likely to have selected ideas from a whole range of options. In a plan like this the choir of the canons would have extended down below the central tower, and possibly into the eastern bay of the nave as well.

The most striking feature of this earliest part of the building is the design of the aisled section of the eastern limb (16). This has been modified by the later addition of a disproportionately tall clearstorey but, although there is certainly evidence of an earlier clearstorey having been started, it is possible that the original design was for only two storeys. These two storeys were jointly embraced by giant arches carried on great cylindrical piers, with the openings into both the aisles and the galleries slotted within those giant arches. This was a type of design which had probably originated in the choir of Tewkesbury Abbey in Gloucestershire, and which was later developed at Romsey Abbey in Hampshire, Oxford Priory (later the cathedral there) and Glastonbury Abbey in Somerset. It must, however, be remembered that there may have been other churches of the same type among the many that have been lost.

Some of the details of Jedburgh suggest the masons may have been brought directly from Tewkesbury. But it is very likely that David was inspired to copy this type of design by Romsey, since he almost certainly saw that church when it was in the course of construction.

16 (Left) *The north side of the choir in Jedburgh Abbey church. The stump of the presbytery as rebuilt some decades later is to its right.*

This was because in 1100 he and his sister Matilda had gone to stay there when she went south to marry Henry I, at which time their aunt Christina, a sister of St Margaret, was a nun of Romsey. He would presumably have maintained his connections with his aunt's abbey throughout the years he spent in England.

Although Dunfermline, Kelso and Jedburgh have the most extensive architectural remains of the monastic churches built for David, reference must also be made here to one of the Cistercian churches built during his reign. The first church of Melrose (**17**) is now known almost entirely from excava-

tions, but it was clearly a building of great significance for the early twelfth-century monastic revival, and had an important place in David's affections. Set not far from the site of an earlier Anglian monastery, its first colony of monks was brought from the Yorkshire abbey of Rievaulx in 1136, which had recently been founded by a land-holder with whom David had a close connection during his years spent in England. It was also at Rievaulx that a favourite member of David's household, Ailred, became a novice and eventually abbot. It may be added that, during Ailred's abbacy David's own step-son, St Waltheof, was to join the Cistercian order at Rievaulx, and he eventually became the second abbot of Melrose. Clearly the Scottish royal house had strong links with Rievaulx, and it is hardly surprising that it should have been there that David looked for guidance in

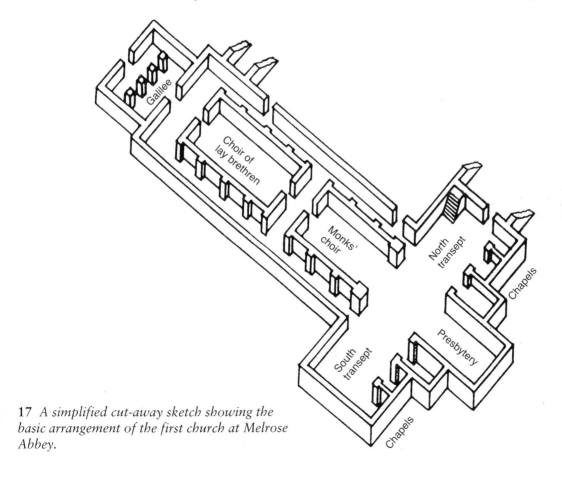

17 *A simplified cut-away sketch showing the basic arrangement of the first church at Melrose Abbey.*

founding his first Cistercian abbey.

However, the plan that was excavated in 1923 shows the first church had closer architectural links with another Yorkshire abbey, that of Fountains. Like most of the earlier Cistercian churches Melrose was architecturally very austere, as is now seen best in the fragmentary remains of the west front, which had no decoration either to the central doorway or to the flat pilasters which buttressed the wall. As part of the pursuit of simplicity many of these churches followed a similar basic plan, which had been first worked out in Burgundy, although the size could vary considerably. There was a rectangular presbytery for the high altar, followed by transepts with chapels on their eastern face to house the altars needed by the priest-monks. West of this was the nave, which was entirely filled by two choirs: one at the east end for the monks themselves, and another further west for the lay brethren, who carried out much of the physical work of the community. No space was needed for layfolk, who were not allowed to take part in the worship of Cistercian communities in the order's earlier years. Melrose conformed to this basic plan, and had a nave of nine bays with an aisle down each side, and three chapels opening off each transept. What is unusual about Melrose, however, is that the inner chapel on each side of the presbytery projects further east than the others, creating a stepped plan; this is very like the plan which is known to have existed at Fountains, but at few other Cistercian churches. Another frequently-found feature in churches of the order was a shallow porch known as a Galilee, which extended across the whole of the west front and accommodated the Sunday procession around the monastic buildings on re-entering the church. At Melrose the Galilee was a slightly later addition, and was both deeper and less wide than usual.

Considering all the links that David I had with monastic houses in England that have been referred to above, we can appreciate why he also had such a wide knowledge of English monastic architecture, and how, on his return to Scotland, he was able to introduce both the newest ideas on monasticism and also the most advanced architectural developments. Scotland's medieval church was indeed fortunate in having such a patron, whatever his penurious successors may have thought to the contrary.

CHAPTER THREE

Monasteries of the Later Twelfth Century

The continuing foundation of monasteries

No one was ever to be quite so magnificently open-handed to the religious orders in Scotland as had been David I. Nevertheless, for some years to come patronage of them was regarded as an essential part of the role of the monarch and his greater subjects. Such activity was not simply an expression of piety, though it was certainly that – but it also provided the family of its founder with a burial place, where it was assumed that prayers would be offered for their souls for all time to come. In addition, a monastery was an expression of the high social standing of the founder, since the act of foundation necessitated the permanent provision of major endowments; it was also a civilizing influence within the estates of the founder.

A number of major monasteries were founded in the later decades of the twelfth century, while others founded in the time of David I were either housed in grand buildings for the first time or had their building operations continued. The greatest of the abbeys set up at this time, at Arbroath, was founded for the Tironensians in 1178 by William the Lion, and was destined to be his own burial place. It was established following a ghostly intervention by Archbishop Thomas Becket, which resulted in the capture of William the Lion on a raid into England at the very moment that Henry II was performing penance at the saintly archbishop's tomb for his part in Becket's murder. (Such were the factors which might lie behind major acts of beneficence!) Further – but smaller – houses were also founded for the Tironensians at Kilwinning and Lindores.

The other orders also continued to flourish. The Cluniacs were provided with their first priory in Scotland at Renfrew in about 1163, a house that was moved to Paisley some six years later. Among the most significant foundations at this period were more for the Cistercians. Coupar Angus was established by Malcolm the Maiden in about 1162, and eventually surpassed even Melrose in wealth, while a smaller house was founded in Wigtonshire at Glenluce in the early 1190s, probably by Roland of Galloway, Constable of Scotland.

One of the more unusual foundations was a priory of Premonstratensian canons as the chapter of the cathedral church of Whithorn, around the 1170s. By this stage it was far more usual for a cathedral to have a staff of secular clergy and, in any case, the strict Premonstratensians could never have been an obvious choice for a cathedral chapter. Perhaps it was an attempt to introduce a more fully regulated way of life, by replacing an existing community of canons with others from nearby Soulseat.

The architecture of the monastic churches in the later twelfth century

The churches built for David I had shown remarkable architectural variety, but were all essentially in the Romanesque – or Scoto-Norman – style of architecture. In such buildings it was a part of the aesthetic approach that there should be a strong sense of the weight of the masonry, and characteristic motifs were semicircular arches and massive, basically cylindrical, columns.

By the later twelfth century, however, new architectural ideas were coming into circulation. In buildings designed at this period we find the masonry being treated in a way which made it seem altogether less ponderous. The mouldings which gave emphasis to the individual features became thinner, more deeply undercut, and thus rather linear in appearance, with sharp contrasts between light and shade. Beyond this, the way in which such mouldings were used to divide up the walls both horizontally and vertically into compartments tended to make the surfaces appear subordinate to the articulation. All of this resulted in a lighter, almost engineered appearance to the structure. At the same time major piers were increasingly composed of what looked like bundles of shafts, some of which might be keeled (pointed) so that, although they were often physically just as massive as equivalent Romanesque piers, the appearance was much less so. In parallel with all of this was a growing use of pointed arches in many situations. It is in these changes that we see the beginnings of the transition from Romanesque to the type of architecture known as Gothic.

A particularly important contribution to these changes was made by the Cistercians, which might seem rather surprising for a monastic order which rejected architectural display. However, as part of the effort to achieve some uniformity of standards through-out the order, the planning and architectural details worked out for its churches around the order's birth place in Burgundy were taken as a starting point for many of the earlier generations of their churches in other countries. Among those exported architectural details were pointed arches and bundled-shaft piers, while the conscious exclusion of unnecessary decoration in the early Cistercian churches was also influential. Some of these elements were taken up in northern England, an area where the order expanded rapidly, and from there they influenced developments in Scotland. That does not mean that the northern English Cistercian churches were straight copies of the Burgundian churches, nor is it to say that those churches were themselves early Gothic. But the introduction of such architectural ideas was to be very important in creating a climate in which the type of Gothic architecture that was to be favoured in Scotland and northern England could take root and develop.

St Andrews Cathedral

The first and most important Scottish building in which these ideas had their early development was the new cathedral priory church at St Andrews, which was started by Bishop Arnold during his short episcopate of between 1160 and 1161, and which was to be the largest church ever built in Scotland (**colour plate 8**). Following on from St Andrews was a group of buildings which included the abbeys of Jedburgh and Arbroath in Scotland, and the priories of Hexham and Lanercost in northern England. This reminds us, incidentally, that the architectural interrelationships between Lowland Scotland and northern England were of the greatest importance at this time and were to remain so for many years to come, though Scotland was to become increasingly a contributor to the pool of ideas and not just a borrower from it. Perversely, however, for all

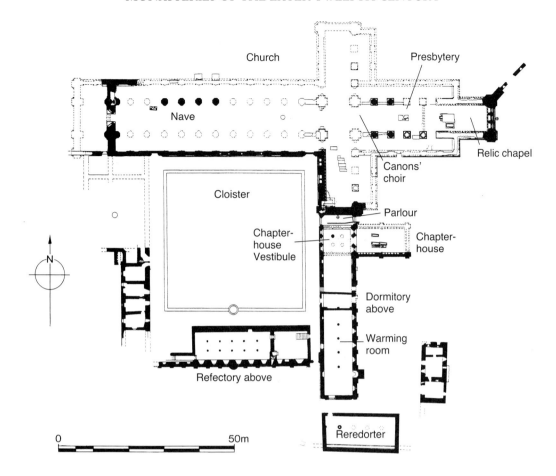

Church

Presbytery

Nave

Relic chapel

Canons' choir

Cloister

Parlour

Chapter-house Vestibule

Chapter-house

Dormitory above

Warming room

Refectory above

Reredorter

N

0   50m

18 *The plan of the cathedral church and priory at St Andrews.*

their architectural debts to the Cistercians, none of these churches belonged to that order; apart from Tironensian Arbroath, the others were Augustinian.

The basic plan of St Andrews is of a type that was to become relatively common in the area that covered northern England and southern Scotland, and was a larger-scale variant on what had already been started at Jedburgh (**18**). At the far end of the eastern limb is an unaisled section, of two bays, with a longer aisled section of six bays to its west. At St Andrews, however, the whole of the eastern limb – and not just the aisles – was covered by stone vaulting. This was very

ambitious for a Scottish church of this period, though it is possible that the vault over the high main space – together with the clearstorey stage that went with it – was an after-thought. Separating the eastern limb from the nave are transepts with three chapels on the eastern face of each. The nave was probably planned to have fourteen bays, but was eventually truncated to twelve after the west front collapsed in the 1270s. (This may have been in 1272, when the *Scotichronicon* records a major storm that damaged Arbroath Abbey and other churches.)

In this arrangement the altar was probably intended to be in the unaisled section at the eastern end, where it would be lit by windows on three sides; eventually, however, it seems this part served as a chapel for the cathedral's relics (**19**). Even so, since the

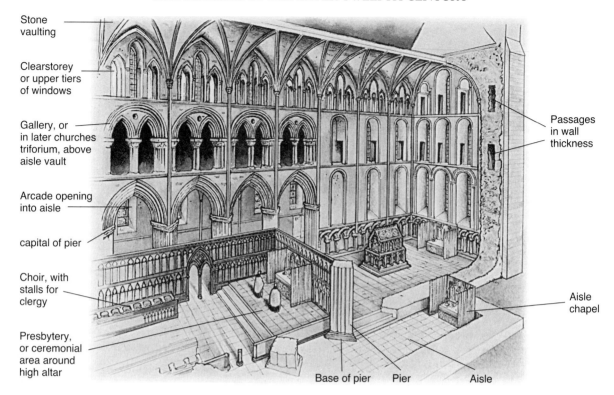

Stone vaulting

Clearstorey or upper tiers of windows

Gallery, or in later churches triforium, above aisle vault

Arcade opening into aisle

capital of pier

Choir, with stalls for clergy

Presbytery, or ceremonial area around high altar

Passages in wall thickness

Aisle chapel

Base of pier   Pier   Aisle

19 *Cut-away sketch of the eastern parts of St Andrews Cathedral. The relic chapel is at the far east end, with the presbytery and choir to its west.*

eastern limb was so long, it is possible the choir stalls for the canons were fully contained within the eastern limb, and did not extend down below the central tower, as might have been expected at this period. Such an enormous cathedral was more expensive than Scotland could easily afford, and it was not to be until 1318 that it was eventually dedicated. The eastern limb may have been complete by the 1230s, however, since Bishop Malvoisin was buried within it in 1238.

In the design of these first parts we can detect a considerable range of influences. The lower walls of the unaisled sections of the eastern limb and transept were decorated with elaborate intersecting decorative arcading, only traces of which still remain on the

east wall, but which still survives in the south transept (**20**). In this we see an approach to design that is still essentially Romanesque and, on first glance, it might also be thought that the original design of the east gable wall was similarly Romanesque. Before remodelling in the fifteenth century, that wall was pierced by rows of three round-headed windows at the three levels of the main elevations, and such an arrangement had already been found in several of the great Romanesque cathedrals of England. Yet this simple tiered arrangement was also favoured by the northern English Cistercians, as can be seen in the transepts of Kirkstall Abbey, and it was probably from such more recent works that the idea was drawn for St Andrews. Certainly several other ideas found at St Andrews must have come from the English Cistercians.

The most obvious of these Cistercian-inspired ideas is the design of the piers, which have the appearance of being made up

21 *One of the Cistercian-inspired water-leaf capitals of the earlier phases of the work at St Andrews Cathedral.*

20 *(Above) The surviving lower part of the west wall of the south transept at St Andrews Cathedral. Although all shafts have been lost, the complex intersecting arcading at the lower level, and the simpler arcading that embraced the windows at the upper level, are still clearly evident.*

of bundles of eight shafts, those facing the four main directions being given additional emphasis by being keeled (pointed). Similar piers had earlier been in vogue in eastern France, and had been taken up by the Cistercians in Burgundy, in the chapter-house at Fontenay for example. Shortly before St Andrews had been started they had also been used in a simpler form in the nave of Kirkstall Abbey, and it could have been those that inspired St Andrews.

Another idea of Cistercian origin can be seen in some of the shaft capitals, which are of a type known as water-leaf (**21**). In its

22 *The crocket capital of one of the vaulting shafts in the south nave aisle at St Andrews Cathedral. The capitals of the main piers were originally a larger version of this.*

plainer versions such caps offered one of the simplest means of making the transition between the circular section of the supporting shaft and the basically square section of the supported arch: the leaves were little more than flattened shapes, with a small inward curl at the top corners. The Burgundian Cistercians used these capitals widely, they were then quickly repeated in the northern English houses of the order, and from there the idea reached St Andrews. There is a similar aesthetic approach in the capitals of the main arcade piers, which had heavy knobs of foliage, known as crockets, at the angles, though a Cistercian debt here is less likely (**22**).

The nave of Jedburgh Abbey

The design of the internal elevations at St Andrews is uncertain since so much has been lost, but we know its relative proportions, and it is likely that it looked rather like what is still visible on a smaller scale in the nave of Jedburgh Abbey (**23**, **24** and **colour plate 3**). There work was probably under way in the last quarter of the century. At both churches

the arcades were carried on piers made up of bundles of eight shafts, although at Jedburgh all eight shafts were keeled rather than just those facing the four cardinal directions. Also at both the gallery stage was rather high – only a little less high than the arcade stage – and it is possible that, as at Jedburgh, the gallery of St Andrews was divided into two smaller pointed arches within a single semi-circular arch.

The main difference between the two was at clearstorey level, and at both that stage seems to have been designed quite late in the operation. At St Andrews each bay of the clearstorey had a single pointed window, flanked by lower arches opening on to the mural passage towards the inside, while on the outside there was a decorative blind arch flanking the window on each side. The

23 *The nave of Jedburgh Abbey church, looking eastwards.*

24 *The plan of Jedburgh Abbey church.*

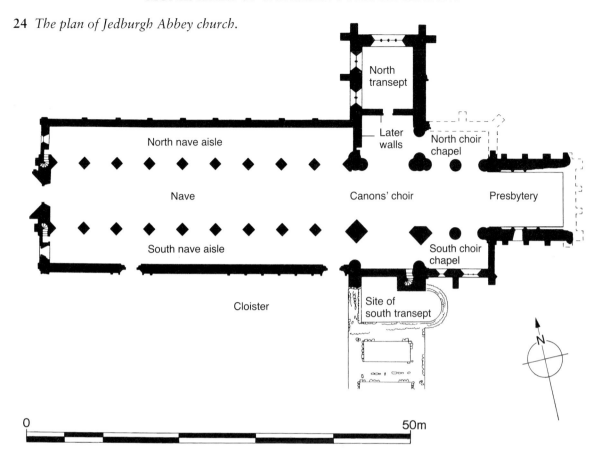

design was like this to accommodate the curve of the vault internally. At Jedburgh, however, there was no high vault, and there was space for two windows to each bay of the clearstorey; externally those two windows were flanked on each side by a blind arch of the same height, rather as at St Andrews, while internally there were four equal-height arches to each bay.

Despite the close similarities between Jedburgh and St Andrews, except at clearstorey level, Jedburgh also shows an awareness of several other buildings. In the arcade capitals, for example, which have lushly enriched water-leaf and crocket foliage that has moved on a long way from earlier Cistercian ideas of simplicity, there are parallels with those at the Cistercian abbey of Byland in north Yorkshire (25). Parallels closer to home may be seen in the design of the west

25 *One of the nave arcade capitals in Jedburgh Abbey church. The basic water-leaf form has been considerably enriched.*

front, where the single large window flanked by decorative arcading shows similarities with the recently completed west front of Kelso Abbey.

Arbroath Abbey

As has already been said, Arbroath is the most architecturally ambitious abbey that we know to have been started in the later twelfth century, presumably once the munificent endowments of William the Lion had been allowed to accumulate. Although there is rougher masonry in the south wall of the nave below the level of the windows, which could indicate that a smaller church had been started at the time of the foundation in 1178, work on the present building can hardly have begun before the last years of the century.

Like Jedburgh, the building owes much to St Andrews. This is first seen in the plan, which is a slightly smaller version of that at the cathedral, albeit with only three bays to the aisled section of the eastern limb, two chapels off each of the transepts, and nine bays to the nave (26). The similarities are even seen in the rather curious way that the ends of the transept chapels are slightly inset from the main gable walls of the transepts. The main difference is that Arbroath had three towers, one at the crossing and two at the west end, though it is possible that the same was intended for St Andrews before the decision was taken to shorten the nave.

The similarities between the two buildings are also seen in the overall design. The tiered triplets of windows in the east gable at Arbroath must surely have been inspired by

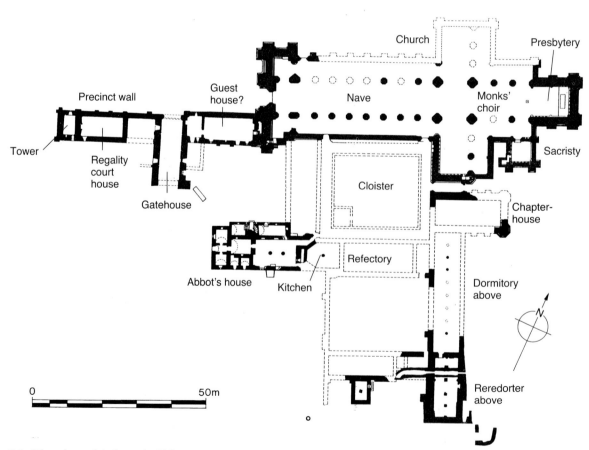

26 *The plan of Arbroath Abbey.*

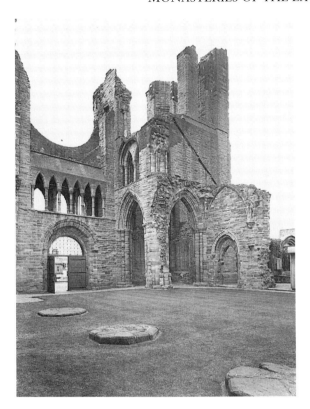

27 *The north-west corner of the nave of Arbroath Abbey church. The original arrangement of the internal three-storeyed elevation is seen most clearly here, at the base of one of the three towers.*

St Andrews – even if at Arbroath the windows are pointed in the newer fashion – and the three-storeyed elevations of the main spaces are also similar (27). Again there are piers of eight shafts, all of which are pointed as at Jedburgh, and the openings of the gallery stage also have pairs of pointed arches within a semicircular arch. However, more recent fashions have prevailed in the way the gallery is relatively less tall in relation to the arcade. We cannot be certain about the design of the clearstorey, since those fragments of it that survive are not typical, but there may have been two windows in each bay at this level.

Yet, as with the relationship between St

Andrews and Jedburgh, no self-respecting master mason was content simply to take ideas from one building, and we find much that is new at Arbroath. One of the most impressive parts of the surviving design is the inner face of the south transept gable wall (28). At the lower level, corresponding to the arcade storey, are three tiers of decorative arches. The two lower rows are both pointed, while the third row, which opens on to a mural passage, has round-headed arches. Above these is a pair of enormously tall pointed windows, rising through the combined height of the gallery and the clearstorey, and in the gable itself is a great circular window. Looking beyond the complexity of this design, it is interesting to see that

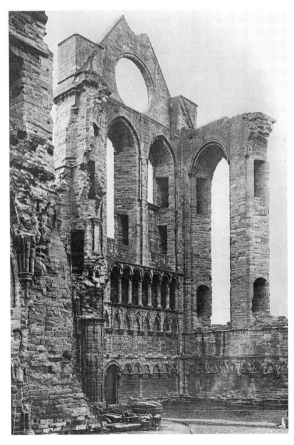

28 *The south transept of Arbroath Abbey church, showing the tiers of decorative arcading.*

round and pointed arches are used almost interchangeably, and this was to be the case for some years into the thirteenth century.

Another area of architectural display was at the base of the western towers, where the mason introduced two levels of decorative arches, with the shafts of the upper tier passing in front of the arches of the lower tier. Related syncopated arcading had been used at Lincoln Cathedral from about 1192, and it may have been from there the idea was taken. But in the overall design of the west front, with its twin towers to either side of a great processional entrance surmounted first by a ceremonial gallery and then by a great circular window, it is possible there could have been some French inspiration (29). It is

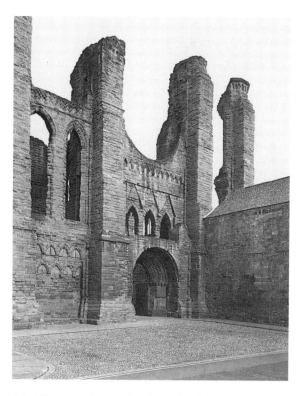

29 *The west front of Arbroath Abbey church. The combination of two towers and a great circular window must have been highly impressive. Traces of the two-tiered decorative arcading are visible at the base of the north tower.*

true that twin-towered facades had become relatively common in England, and there were also precedents for the circular window at such as Byland, so the two ideas could simply have been combined from different English sources. However, the combination of these elements was also being explored in France around this time, as at Laon Cathedral, for example, where the west front was started around 1190. If it seems strange to suggest French inspiration, it must be remembered that the early abbots maintained close contacts with the mother house in France, and are likely to have seen much that was being built there at the time.

The architectural details of Arbroath are sadly decayed. But several show parallels with those in the eastern limb of the priory church of Hexham in Northumberland, a building that was rising around the same years as Arbroath. Apart from overall similarities of design and proportion, they share details such as a half pier in the form of a semi-octagon with sunken shafts at the angles. They also have a newer type of foliage decoration, known as stiff-leaf, in common. Foliage of this sort usually has three formalized lobes to each sprig, which tend to spread out in windswept interlocking patterns. Such foliage was to remain in fashion for around a century, from the later 1100s onwards, and will be found in a number of the buildings considered below.

Some Cistercian abbeys

In following the strand of ideas which connects St Andrews, the nave of Jedburgh and Arbroath, we have moved forward rather quickly, and must now go back to consider other churches under construction in the later twelfth century. Not unnaturally at a period when ideas introduced into Britain by the Cistercian order were so influential, a number of the more important Scottish buildings at this time were also Cistercian.

30 *The plan of Dundrennan Abbey.*

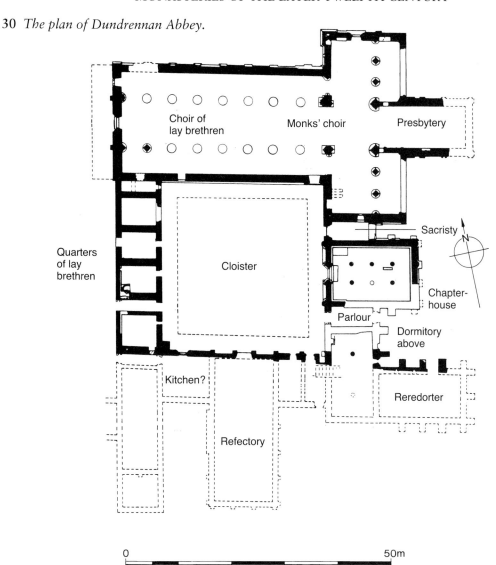

Choir of lay brethren

Monks' choir

Presbytery

Quarters of lay brethren

Cloister

Sacristy

N

Chapter-house

Parlour

Dormitory above

Kitchen?

Reredorter

Refectory

0   50m

The most impressive of these Cistercian churches is that of Dundrennan (**30** and **colour plate 4**). It had been set out to the characteristic plan of the order around the time of its foundation in 1142, but the interior of the transepts was grandly remodelled in the later decades of the century. By that stage the austerity of the order's earliest ideals was being diluted; this is seen most obviously in the three-storeyed design, since the Cistercians had earlier tended to reject the middle storey as a purely decorative feature. Rather curiously, at Dundrennan the design of this stage differs between the two transepts, with four blind arches to each bay in the north transept and two open arches in the other (**31**). Nevertheless, many of the familiar features associated with the order are still to be seen, including bundled-shaft piers. The capitals to those piers are as simple as they could possibly be, having no more than a flared bell to make the transition from shaft to arch. (Such caps are known as chalice caps because of their shape.) Analysis of the details shows that many of the elements used here were derived from English sister

45

houses, including Roche in Nottinghamshire and Byland in Yorkshire. Despite some slight awkwardnesses, which may have resulted from the attempt to remodel an earlier structure, the results are highly effective.

Some of the same details as at Dundrennan are to be found in another Cistercian house in the same region, that of Glenluce, which was founded around 1190. There is the same basic plan, and bundled-shaft piers were also used. But Glenluce was a much smaller house and never aspired to the three-storeyed splendours of Dundrennan. Bundled-shaft piers were yet again used in the order's most northerly house, at Kinloss, which had been founded in about 1150, but where major rebuilding probably started towards the end of the century. However, at some stage Kinloss acquired a plan which was most unusual for a Cistercian house in Scotland, in having aisles which extended the full length of the eastern limb. Unfortunately so little remains that we cannot be certain when this was done.

A more complex plan was also adopted at Newbattle in Midlothian, another of the order's major houses. There our understanding of the plan is based on inadequate excavations carried out towards the end of the last century, which revealed that aisles extended the length of the short eastern limb. However, the easternmost piers appear to have been of similarly massive scale as the crossing piers, which has led to the suggestion that they supported a high gable wall, with lower chapels to the east of that wall. This was a plan type that had originated in England in the early twelfth century, but which became particularly popular with the Cistercians. The earliest Cistercian version of the plan could have been at Morimond in Champagne, built about 1160, but the immediate inspiration for Newbattle was perhaps

Byland Abbey, in Yorkshire, The long ten-bay aisled nave of Newbattle was probably only completed in the thirteenth century, on the indications of the widely-projecting buttresses; there is known to have been a dedication in 1233.

Abbeys which followed Cistercian planning

As already discussed, architectural details introduced by the Cistercians into northern England – such as the design of piers and capitals, and perhaps also the early use of pointed arches – were highly influential. This was also true of Cistercian planning. The simple plans used by the order with the intention of avoiding architectural display were also relatively cheap to build, and were attractive for other houses that could not afford expensive buildings. In fact, not even the greatest Scottish abbeys were able to indulge in the most complex types of planning favoured elsewhere, such as those in which a semicircular or polygonal aisle passed around an apse and from which a series of smaller chapels radiated, so it is hardly surprising that simpler plans were preferred in the smaller houses.

The Tironensian house of Lindores, in Fife, was probably started around the time of its foundation around 1190, though construction must have extended well into the following century. It is now in a very ruined state, but the plan of the eastern limb and transept was clearly similar to that of Dundrennan, with its short rectangular presbytery and three chapels on each transept. It also seems the piers were of the bundled-shaft type, since the responds (half-piers) at the ends of the transept arcades are like this. The nave of Lindores has a single aisle on the side away from the cloister but as is often the case with such aisles, it seems it was a later addition to an originally aisle-less nave. The main reason for assuming this is that it stops short of the

31 The north transept of Dundrennan Abbey.

free-standing campanile (bell tower), at the north-west angle of the nave, in a way that is hard to explain otherwise.

There was a similar plan at the Augustinian abbey of Cambuskenneth in Stirlingshire, which is even more extensively destroyed than Lindores, but which is similarly likely to have been started at the end of the twelfth century and completed in the following. In this case there were only two chapels on the east face of each transept, but here again there is a single north aisle, on the side away from the cloister. In this case the possibility that the aisle was an addition is indicated by the way the shafts which divide the south wall into bays follow a different rhythm from the arcade piers and wall shafts on the north side. Cambuskenneth is again like Lindores in having a free-standing campanile to the north of the west front, but here it was a rather later addition, and is sited well clear of the north aisle.

Some other later twelfth-century building operations

Several other significant campaigns were started or continued in the later decades of the century, though in some cases so little remains that we cannot understand how they formed part of the overall scheme. At Paisley Abbey, for example, the earliest fragment that is still in place, the round-arched south-east doorway from the nave into the cloister, must be of this period. It has capitals of fleshy crocket form or with simple stiff-leaf foliage.

The variety of foliage decoration on the capitals is often one of the great delights of buildings at this period. The continuing work on the nave of Kelso Abbey is a particularly useful indicator of changing fashions, since it was built one layer at a time (32). Thus the triforium stage, above the arcade, still has mainly scallop caps like those of the arcade, and they are carried on cylindrical shafts. But some water-leaf caps are also introduced at

32 *The south nave wall at Kelso Abbey. The lack of correspondence between the rhythm of the three storeys is clearly evident.*

this level. By the time the clearstorey is reached the small piers have triplets of shafts with capitals mainly of water-leaf type, but with some scallops still mixed in, and also some crockets. The next stage up is the mural passage in the west tower, immediately above the crossing arches, where there are chalice capitals like those at Dundrennan.

If at Kelso we see late twelfth-century capitals in their most austere form, around the same time we can find more lavish developments on these same ideas at Holyrood. The simple first church that had been built there soon proved inadequate for the ambitions of the community, and work on a larger building was started around the last decade of the century. Since there are only fragmentary foundations of the eastern limb we do not know where the work started. But in the

1 *The stone cells at Eileach-an-Naoimh.*

2 *The choir and presbytery of Jedburgh Abbey church, as it could have appeared by the late twelfth century (Harry Bland).*

3 *Jedburgh Abbey church from the south. The nave is to the left and the choir to the right.*

4 *The transepts of Dundrennan Abbey church, viewed across the cloister. The chapter-house entrance is on the right.*

5   *The freestanding bell-tower of Cambuskenneth Abbey, with Stirling Castle in the background.*

6   *Crossraguel Abbey church from the north-west. The nave is to the right, with the choir and presbytery beyond the gable wall to the right.*

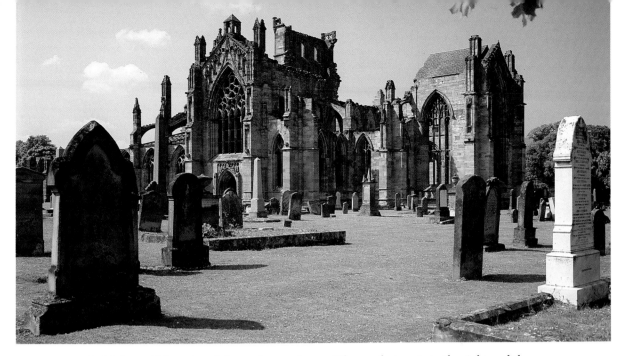

7 *Melrose Abbey church from the south-east. The presbytery is to the right and the south transept projects to its left.*

8 *A cut-away reconstruction sketch of the cathedral church and the main core of priory buildings at St Andrews (David Simon).*

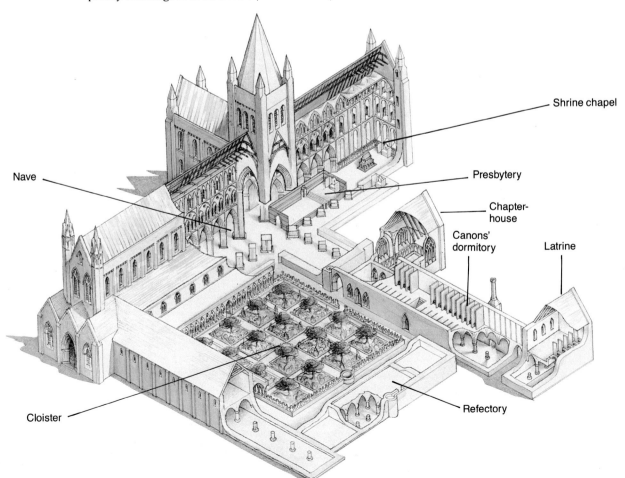

Shrine chapel

Nave

Presbytery

Chapter-house

Canons' dormitory

Latrine

Cloister

Refectory

9 *The east range of monastic buildings, viewed from across the cloister, at Dryburgh Abbey.*

10 *The monastic buildings at Dunfermline Abbey. The gatehouse and refectory are to the left, and the undercrofts of the east range and latrine block to the right.*

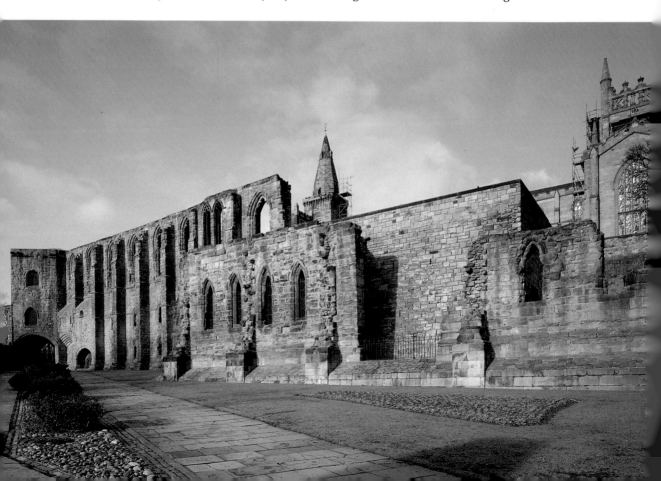

11 *An aerial view of the precinct of Dunfermline Abbey from the south-east. The church is at the centre, with the guest house and refectory to its left.*

12 *An aerial view of Inchmahome Priory, in the lake of Menteith, from the south.*

13 *An aerial view of Inchcolm Abbey, in the Firth of Forth, from the north. The earlier church is to the right, and the outline of the later church to the left, with the monastic buildings behind.*

14 *A model showing how Jedburgh Abbey probably looked on the eve of the Reformation, viewed from the south-west.*

15 *The precinct wall and harbour gate of St Andrews Cathedral Priory. The tower of St Rule's church and the east gable of the cathedral rise in the background to the right.*

33 *The north nave wall at Holyrood Abbey church.*

nave it began with a new north aisle well beyond the existing church, so that the church could remain in use while building went on around it (33). The earliest part to be built was, of course, the level below the windows, and internally the dado there has an even more elaborate display of intersect-ing arcading than at St Andrews. Most of its caps are of enriched water-leaf and crocket types, although with additional decoration that includes a form of stiff-leaf. By the time the west bay was reached the stiff-leaf foliage was being treated more freely, and this was even more the case when work began at the level of the aisle windows. On the vaulting shafts and the smaller shafts which flank the windows, there are particularly luxuriant growths of stiff-leaf, sometimes combined with richly convoluted water-leaves.

The choir of Coldingham and the presbytery of Jedburgh

Another place where there are similarly lush growths of sculpted foliage is the choir of the Benedictine priory of Coldingham in Berwickshire, where the choir was rebuilt to an aisle-less rectangular plan that was slightly longer and wider than its predecessor. Internally the new choir was divided into two levels (34). At the lower level is wall arcading, while at the upper level there is a wall passage running in front of the windows; it has an arcade towards the interior with tall arches corresponding to the windows and lower arches between. Such a design belongs within an architectural group

34 *The north choir wall at Coldingham Priory church.*

which also includes the nave of Ripon Minster (a collegiate church) and Nun Monkton nunnery church, both in Yorkshire, together with the choir of St Bees in Cumberland. Decorating the capitals of the upper arcade is a rich variety of foliage, including crockets, water-leaf and stiff-leaf and, although the quality varies, they merit close inspection.

One other building which may belong to the same group as Coldingham is the rebuilt presbytery of Jedburgh (see **16** and **colour plate 2**). Only the stumps of this now remain, where they adjoin the aisled sections of the choir. But early views suggest there was something similar to what is still visible at Coldingham, with decorative wall arcading at the lower level, and an open arcade in front of the wall passage at the upper level, which steps up and down to accommodate the windows. Eventually both the choir and the presbytery were capped by an inappropriately tall clearstorey which raised the wall-head to the same height as in the nave. Rather intriguingly, there are also signs of an earlier clearstorey having been started before that one was built, which could suggest the new presbytery was always intended to have a clearstorey. However, it is equally possible that the earlier and lower clearstorey was started only a little before the one that was eventually built, and that it was abandoned soon after being started when the decision was taken to raise the eastern limb to the same height as the nave. If so, the original design for the extended presbytery would have been very like the choir of Coldingham.

The last phase of this series of campaigns at Jedburgh is probably represented by the completion of the nave clearstorey, which has already been discussed. But by then the thirteenth century had begun, and we move into a new phase of Scottish monastic architecture.

CHAPTER FOUR

The Religious Life

Having considered the Scottish monasteries in the course of the twelfth century when they were at the height of their influence, this is probably an appropriate stage to make a digression to consider the way of life followed by the members of such communities.

The daily round for those who dedicated themselves to life in a medieval community of monks, canons or even of friars, was not as unchanging as is often thought. Not only were there differences between the various orders, but much depended on the time of year or the importance of a particular feast day, while other changes inevitably crept in over a period of time. In a small book like this it would not be possible to give more than the briefest indication of the range of possibilities. We shall instead concentrate on what may be regarded as a norm in the classic age of Scottish monasticism – in the twelfth and early thirteenth centuries – and make only brief reference to the changes that are known to have been introduced at later stages. But it must be remembered that even aspects of the basic monastic commitments could be interpreted in different ways with the passage of time.

The members of the community

The range of individuals who made up a religious community might vary considerably (35). St Benedict had visualized that there would be two main types of entrant: the oblates and the novices. The former were boys who were given to the house by their parents, and who were eventually accepted as full members of the community when they reached maturity; the latter were those who joined the house on reaching maturity, and

35 *A Benedictine monk (Dugdale's* Monasticon).

who became full members after a period of probation. The tendency was, however, for it to be seen as increasingly unacceptable for children to be placed in a community with no choice on their part, and by the twelfth century most monks entered the monastic life of their own free will.

It is difficult to be certain how wide a social gamut would be represented in a monastery. While there is little to suggest that any Scottish houses were the exclusive abode of the sons of aristocratic families – as was the case in some houses on the Continent – monks and canons usually had to be of at least free birth. Beyond that, it is perhaps more likely that the middle and upper social strata were better represented than the lower. The friars may have been rather more democratic, though even with them there was probably a need for a new entrant to bring some form of endowment with him.

In several orders there were also members known as *conversi* or lay brethren, who carried out much of the manual labour. They lacked the education to participate fully in the Latin services, and were therefore excused attendance at some, so that they had time for all the work expected of them. Some of these would have entered their communities relatively late in life and are likely to have been illiterate, but it is also probable that many were of relatively low social origins. The order that made most use of such *conversi*, the Cistercians, was able to draw them in such vast numbers in its heyday that enormous buildings had to be provided to house them. However, by the fourteenth century, when the Cistercians were beginning to differ little from the other orders, recruitment of *conversi* dried up, and reliance was placed on paid servants to carry out the menial work within the precinct, and to do much of the labour on the outlying estates.

The corporate worship of the community

Following the exhortation of the psalmist, monks worshipped the Lord seven times daily. Their services, made up of psalms, prayers, antiphons and readings, constituted the *opus dei* (work of God), or canonical hours. In the monastery of an order that had neither over-embellished its services, such as the Cluniacs, nor cut them back dramatically, like some of the friars, during the summer season on a day that was not a special feast the services would probably start at about two o'clock in the morning (36).

The night-time service of Nocturns (later known as Matins) was followed at about

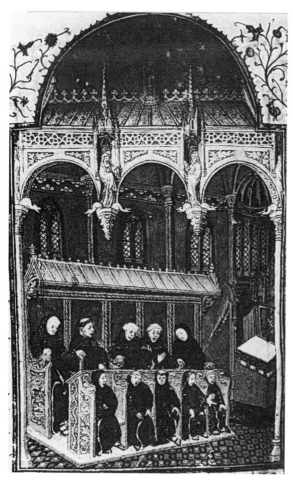

36 *A service in a monastic choir (by permission, British Library Cotton Dom. AXVII f.122v.).*

half past three by Matins (later known as Lauds), and there may then have been a period of rest before the first daytime service of Prime at around six o'clock. Terce came at eight o'clock, Sext at about half past eleven, and None around half past two. In the evening Vespers was likely to be about six o'clock and the short final service of Compline was probably at eight. This meant that the summer day lasted from about half past one in the morning until around quarter past eight at night. By contrast, in winter the monks would rise at about half past two and retire at about half past six, after following a more compressed time-table. In addition to the hours there would be corporate celebrations of the mass. By the twelfth century there may have been two such celebrations; in the summer the first of these, the Morrow Mass, would follow Prime, but in the winter it was more likely to follow Terce. It was the main Sung Mass which followed Terce in the summer, whereas in the winter it followed Sext.

Beyond these, however, there was a tendency to the proliferation of masses in the course of the Middle Ages. This was partly because of the growing numbers of monks who were ordained priests, and who were therefore expected to celebrate private masses on a more or less regular basis. But the main reason for this increase was because so many people wished to be buried within monastic churches and to have prayers said for themselves by the monks, canons or friars, or by specially-paid priests. The medieval obsession with the consequences of sin, together with the belief in purgatory, meant there was a great demand for prayers to be said for one's soul in order to increase the chances of salvation and to reduce the suffering that had to be undergone in purgatory.

Benefactors of a monastic house, and particularly the founder and his family, had always expected to be prayed for, and would have the benefit of Obits – masses on the anniversary of their death. Yet this was not enough for many, who instead made arrangements for soul masses to be said until the end of time by a succession of priests at one or more altars or even within specially built chapels, where the donor might also be buried. Such endowments were known as chantries, and many monastic churches came to have large numbers attached to them. By the fourteenth century it is likely that even the Cistercians, who had previously shunned such contacts with the outside world, were permitting them within their churches. The demand for burial in monastic churches partly stemmed from an idea that something of the sanctity of the place must be transferred to those buried within it, but mainly from the belief that the prayers of cloistered monks were particularly efficacious. Indeed, it was believed that one of the surest ways to heaven was to die as a member of a religious community, and some layfolk made elaborate arrangements so that, as death approached, they would be carried to a monastery and clothed in the monastic habit before they died. This was known as becoming a monk *ad succurrendum*, and such arrangements were also likely to include burial within the abbey together with elaborately costly provision for masses.

The daily life of the community

The borderline between worship and everyday life in a monastery was rather blurred, since all activities tended to be ritualized in a way that endowed them with a sacred quality. Even the manner of sleeping was dictated, with the heavy woollen habit still being worn in bed, and the hands folded in a prescribed way above the blanket. Second in importance to the services was the daily meeting called Chapter, which derived its name from the reading of a chapter of the Rule of St Benedict in houses of monks. This took place after the Morrow Mass in the room specially set aside for the purpose. Apart from the reading, the business of the community was discussed, and its members confessed their faults and received correction.

Eating, which took place in the refectory, was imbued with ritual significance because of the analogy between bodily and spiritual sustenance, and readings of an appropriate nature were all that were allowed to break the silence (37). The main meal, the *prandium*, was taken around midday in summer – after Sext – and about two o'clock in winter – after None. For the orders of monks it was essentially vegetarian in content, consisting mainly of bread, vegetables and eggs, though fish was also evidently included from an early date. The orders of canons may have been less strict in this. In summer there would also be a light supper before Vespers and a drink would be permitted after None, while in winter there would be an evening drink before Compline.

It is likely that the rule on vegetarian fare within the monastic refectory remained in force throughout the Middle Ages. However, the monks who were so old or infirm that they had to live within the less rigid regime of the infirmary were allowed meat, and excuses eventually came to be found by the other monks for resorting to the infirmary to enjoy such treats on a number of pretexts. Regular blood-letting, which was regarded as beneficial to the health and which took place in the infirmary, was one such pretext. Meat also had to be allowed elsewhere and, since the head of the community had to entertain guests from the outside world, his house was certainly one place where meat was found on the table, and where selected monks might be invited to enjoy it. Otherwise meat might also be taken in a small dining room known as the misericord, roughly translatable as 'place of mercy'; one of the two dining halls mentioned in an account of Arbroath in 1517 may have been for such use.

37 *A reconstruction sketch of the monastic refectory at Dunfermline Abbey. The high table is on a dais at the far end, from which a doorway led up to the pulpit, marked by the pair of narrow windows.*

It is in the growth of pittances that we see what was perhaps the greatest erosion of original austerity, however. These were treats that were usually provided from special funds set up by benefactors, such as the annual rent which Robert I gave to Melrose in 1326 to allow the community to enjoy a daily helping of rice made with milk of almonds.

Work of various kinds was an essential part of the monastic day, and there might be time for reading before Prime and again before Sext. So far as physical work was concerned, there was a short period for this between Chapter and Terce, though the main period was in the afternoon, between None and supper in summer or between dinner and Vespers in winter. But it is open to debate how far any of this work continued to be physically demanding once the various orders had passed through their phase of initial enthusiasm. The Cistercians had certainly placed great stress on demanding work at first, though the nature of their land-holdings, together with the rules on their own enclosure within the precinct, meant that it was inevitable that most of the farm labouring was carried out by lay brethren, and later by paid servants under the supervision of monks.

Even at a later period, however, there was still scope for gardening and small-scale farming to be conducted by the monks within the precinct, and for many monks this may have been a welcome activity. For others, however, more sedentary pursuits such as reading, writing and meditation were always more conducive to a spiritual frame of mind. In this connection, it must be remembered that, although the production of great illuminated manuscripts was increasingly a lay profession from the thirteenth century onwards, the copying of books continued to

be one of the great contributions to civilization of the monasteries. Among the books copied were the works of the pagan classical authors, some of which might now otherwise be lost.

Most of these more sedentary occupations were meant to be accommodated within the covered walks which extended around the four sides of the cloister (38). The north walk, which was usually in the lee of the church and which also had the advantage of whatever sun might be available, was the favourite place for such activities. But writing must have been impossible even there for much of the Scottish winter, and some of the rooms within the ranges around the cloister were perhaps used for such activities (39). The cloister walks were also the route for the

38 *A view across the cloister at Melrose Abbey. Within the covered walks which used to run around its perimeter the monks would have carried out many of their more sedentary tasks.*

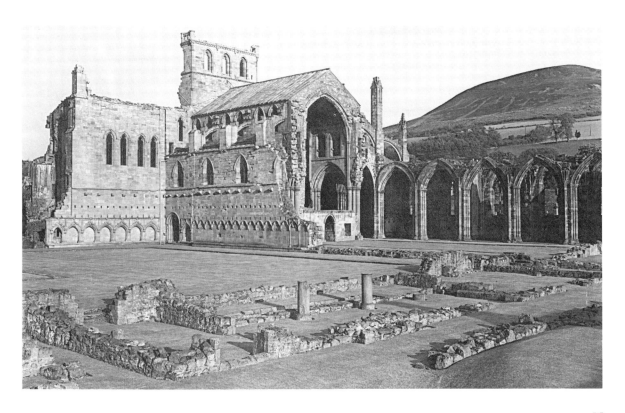

39 *A friar at work in his cell (by permission, British Library Royal 14 E1 vol.1 f.3r.).*

processions which regularly passed around the church and monastic buildings, and they were the setting for the readings from the lives of the fathers, known as the 'Collations' of Cassian, which took place before Compline. In Cistercian houses there was a further use for the cloister as a result of the particular emphasis that was placed on the ritual weekly *mandatum*, or washing of feet, which took place in the cloister walk against the refectory.

All of these activities were as far as possible carried out in silence, though the degree of silence expected varied between the orders and according to the time of day. In all the enclosed orders the greater silence was meant to be observed completely between Compline in the evening and Prime on the following day. Meals were also meant to be silent occasions, and a simple sign language was evolved to permit the basic essential communication. But it seems that necessary speech was allowed within the cloister outside those times, and small spaces known as *locutoria* or parlours were specifically provided off the two sides of the cloister for this purpose. However, since they were usually corridors to the areas outside the cloister, they cannot have been attractive places within which to linger.

Monastic office-holders

It was one of the underlying principles of the monastic life that the monks or canons and their superior should pursue their way of life in common, sharing the same meals and the same sleeping place. This became increasingly difficult, however. The greater abbeys might be enormously wealthy institutions, and with the land which generated much of that wealth went the duties and responsibilities of any other land-holder within the complex system of feudal tenure. As members of a small intellectual élite the heads of these houses were also often called upon by their monarch to serve in the government and administration of the nation. As a consequence, the heads of many houses became increasingly separated from the lives of their communities: they might frequently have to be absent, and when they were at home they were often called upon to provide hospitality for important visitors. Thus, although their residences might be sufficiently close to the other monastic buildings for lip-service to be paid to the idea of the common life, in reality their monks probably saw little enough of them.

This was not all. Administration in all ages has been a wonderfully expansive process, and the efficient running of a great monastery and its possessions came to require the services of many other office holders, known as obedientiaries. Faced with frequent absences by the abbot, the daily administration devolved on the prior, and he might require the services of a sub-prior. Beneath them were many other departments, each headed by its own obedientiary and his assistants. The sacrist was in charge of the vestments and other items required for the services; the chamberlain ensured the brethren had the clothing they needed; the novice master trained candidates for entry; the almoner carried out the practical charity of the monastery; the guest master ensured that guests received hospitality appropriate to their station; the infirmarian was responsible for the old and sick; the cellarer supervised the provisions and drink required for the refectory; the pittancer doled out the culinary treats that became such a feature of the diet of many houses.

All these – and many others in a great monastery – became more and more drawn into the daily round of practical affairs, and inevitably less involved in the purely spiritual side of religious life. Eventually, as many as half of any community might be office holders, and with those offices had to go exemptions from at least some of the church services. All of this was probably in itself harmless enough, though, like a number of other aspects that crept into monastic life, it must have made the highest religious standards less easy to achieve.

Corporate wealth and personal poverty

There is not space here to give detailed consideration to all the possible sources of income of a house of monks or canons, but a little must be said. Looking at a major house such as Dunfermline, it is astonishing to see the range of ways that the founder might endow his new community. Among David I's gifts were lands at Dunfermline, Kinghorn and Inveresk, an eighth of the income from judicial procedures in Fife, properties in five burghs, a proportion of the seals that were taken at Kinghorn, a stipulated portion of the income from produce of various kinds and a part of the revenues he still drew from England. By his death in 1153 he had added further to this, including more lands and portions of other produce, while other benefac-

tors who wished to be associated with the work of supporting the monks provided yet more endowments.

Among other major sources of income, Dunfermline also benefited from the trading activities of the burgh which grew up around its walls, and which was under the abbey's special protection. But a particularly important source of funds for Dunfermline, and for many other monastic houses as well, came from parish churches. In setting up the parochial network it had been arranged that the main way of funding churches should be a teind (a tenth part) of all produce within them, and when a monastery was given a parish it usually also took over most of this income. David I himself started this process for Dunfermline, and eventually the abbey enjoyed the income of at least eighteen parishes in this way. This was greatly to the benefit of the abbeys, but conversely it had a disastrous impact on the appropriated parishes. The appropriating abbeys were supposed to provide for the spiritual welfare of the parishioners by instituting a vicar, but there is considerable evidence that they were frequently unwilling to pay enough to be able to engage priests of sufficient calibre. They were also often reluctant to pay for repairs to the chancel of the appropriated churches, which was the part of the fabric for which they were responsible.

Most monastic houses drew a great deal of wealth from land, much of which would have been given to them in small and scattered parcels by individual donors. This income might come in the form of rents or as produce, with the latter either being sold or used by the community itself. The Cistercian order tended to be particularly successful in the exploitation of land, and sometimes had more consolidated holdings than the other orders because of their willingness to accept untamed wilderness, which they quickly transformed into good farming land. However, the order sometimes gained a reputation for ruthlessness because of the way that existing tenants might be turned away so that the land could be directly exploited by the monasteries as part of their pursuit of self-sufficiency. A speciality of several houses of the order was wool farming, and as early as the twelfth century Melrose was selling its wool in the Low Countries; indeed, that abbey was probably the largest single producer of wool in Scotland and gained additional advantages from the special privileges granted to it by the Count of Flanders in the 1180s.

Income could also be generated from the more religious aspects of monastic life. Those who wished to be buried in an abbey, for example, realized that this was not a cheap option: it apparently cost Sir Alan Mortimer half his estate in 1216 to gain the right of burial in Inchcolm. A house fortunate enough to possess popular relics had yet another invaluable source of income from the pilgrims who came to plead for the saint's aid and intercession. It is thus easy to understand why a monastery should be anxious to further the claims for canonization of any potential candidate, and why alarmingly apocryphal lives might be written as part of the effort to engender enthusiasm for a saint's cult. St Mirren, who is supposed to have founded a monastery at Paisley, and who came to be associated with the medieval abbey there, is just one of a considerable number of rather shadowy saints whose life story seems to have been at least partly copied from those whose life stories are only slightly less insubstantial. At the side of such saints, the greater historical certainties of such as Margaret at Dunfermline and Waltheof at Melrose appear comfortingly substantial.

As a result of all of these – and other – sources of income, most of the greater abbeys were very wealthy indeed. Despite this, many of them lived up to or even beyond their means, and a combination of costly or wasteful administrative structures together with massively expensive building operations left even the wealthiest houses frequently critically short of funds. Nevertheless, once the initial fervour had passed, the life of a monk in one of the larger houses could be very comfortable. There may even have been a tendency to limit new recruits to houses to ensure that the available funds were not too thinly spread, though there was probably less of this in Scotland than elsewhere in Europe.

St Benedict had intended that all of a monastery's property should be held in common, and that monks following his rule should be given what they needed from that common holding. But, surrounded by such wealth it was difficult for the individual monk or canon to continue with the pretence of personal poverty, and in the last centuries of the Middle Ages a system grew up which allowed each monk or canon his personal 'portion' of the monastic income. Attempts were made to eradicate this abuse on a number of occasions, but were hotly resisted, and there was even one case of monks threatening to stay away from choir if their portions were not increased! The idea of the common life was also eroded so far as the accommodation occupied by the monks and canons was concerned, since at several monasteries they came to expect to have their own private chambers or houses, sometimes with gardens attached.

However, it would be unfair to judge medieval monasticism on the basis of the relaxations which inevitably crept in. At its worst it may have become spiritually undemanding and complacent, and may have failed to meet the high expectations of those would-be benefactors whose own endowments in fact made the attainment of high goals less easy to achieve. But at its best, in the days of initial fervour or in later periods of renewal, it should not be forgotten that monasticism demanded complete commitment on the part of its adherents, and that it was one of the most powerful influences on European civilization.

CHAPTER FIVE

The Religious Houses of the Thirteenth Century

The pattern of new foundations

The thirteenth century was a highly productive period for monastic architecture, and it is at the beginning of this century that we see the last vestiges of the Romanesque approach to design being succeeded by Gothic. Yet it is also true that, after the close of the twelfth century, the religious orders were seldom again to be the great driving force within the church they once had been. As their dynamism declined they also began to forfeit some of the interest of lay patrons, which had earlier led to the acquisition of such tremendous endowments. Nevertheless, considerable numbers of new foundations were still being made; indeed, in the later years of Alexander II, around the second quarter of the thirteenth century, there were probably more new foundations than at any other time. What we see, however, is a diminution in the scale of new foundations, together with a shift of enthusiasm towards newer forms of the religious life.

The only important new foundation for the Benedictines in the thirteenth century was Iona, while the Cluniacs gained a new oratory at Crossraguel which, towards the end of the century, grew into an independent abbey. Of the 'reformed' Benedictine orders, the Tironensians acquired minor additional houses at Fogo and Fyvie, while the Cistercians continued to attract the lion's share of new patronage. Further houses were founded for them at Balmerino, Culross, Deer, Saddell and Sweetheart – the last dating from as late as the 1270s.

By this stage the orders of canons may have represented an even more attractive option than before. This was partly because a small house of canons was more affordable than one of monks, since the numbers needed for a viable community were less, and they could be attached to an existing church. At a time when the lay magnates rather than the royal house were responsible for the majority of fresh foundations, this was particularly significant. Thus, in the course of the century, the Augustinians acquired houses at Inchaffray, Inchmahome, Blantyre, Monymusk and Abernethy, most of which were on the sites of earlier communities or attached to existing churches, and many of which were very small. The Premonstratensian canons were also favoured with new foundations at Tongland, Fearn and Holywood.

However, it seems the palates of potential patrons were becoming jaded, and there was a search for newer religious forms. Among these were the Trinitarians, whose life was closer to that of the canons than the monks, and who were established at Berwick, Dunbar, Scotlandwell, Houston, Aberdeen and Peebles in the course of the thirteenth century, while a double house of Gilbertine canons and nuns was planned for Dalmilling near Ayr, but never established. Perhaps the most notable achievements of the century were the introduction in the 1230s both of the Valliscaulian monks and also of the Dominican and Franciscan friars. In each case this was possibly as a result of the direct interest of Alexander II.

With such foundations Scotland showed itself to be still keeping close contacts with European developments. The Valliscaulians represented a return to the first principles of Benedictine monasticism in the way the Cistercians had a century earlier, even if they attracted little patronage outside France and Scotland. The orders of friars were to be particularly important for the future, with their emphasis on an active mission to the urban population, and they continued to attract patronage almost up to the eve of the Reformation. Unfortunately, however, a combination of replacement by later buildings and high losses as a result of their valuable urban sites, means that, with the possible exception of Luffness, we appear to have no mendicant architecture of this period.

The naves of St Andrews and Holyrood

Among the grandest building campaigns under way in the early years of the thirteenth century were the continuing works on the naves of St Andrews and Holyrood. At the former nearly all of the evidence has been lost, apart from the south wall of the nave, and the indications of the relative heights of the three storeys in the west wall that was built at the end of the century. But from these we can at least see that the proportions of the design had changed from those in the choir to bring them into line with newer fashions. The arcades were taller, while the middle stage – which by now should probably be called a triforium rather than a gallery – was relatively shorter. At some stage also the single

round-headed windows in each bay of the aisles were superseded by pointed windows subdivided by Y-tracery, though this change probably did not happen until later in the century.

At Holyrood, the outer wall of the north aisle having been completed, the western towers were laid out next, to an unusual plan which projected them sideways and westwards from the outer corners of the west front (40). The front was thus made as wide as possible, while a recessed area was created between the towers which concentrated emphasis on one of the most impressive and richly decorated processional doorways ever built in Scotland. Work then moved on to the interior of the nave, possibly around the second decade of the century.

The west front and interior of the nave at Holyrood were designed by master masons trained within very different backgrounds from the master who had designed the north aisle wall. The biggest single influence on the design of the interior was the work at Lincoln Cathedral, started towards the end of the previous century (41). Above the lofty arcades was a relatively short triforium stage, which was treated almost as a series of windows, with two arches to each bay, each of which contained two smaller steeply pointed arches, and with a yet smaller arch tucked below each. Between the heads of the pairs of arches, smaller openings were punched through the thin plate of masonry contained by the main arch; such 'plate-tracery' foreshadows the more complex tracery patterns that were to become so important a feature of Gothic churches. Above the triforium, the clearstorey has been destroyed, but from the fragments that remain we know that it was

40 *The west front of Holyrood Abbey church. The northern of the two towers is to the left, but the southern tower is below the palace of the 1670s.*

41 (Left) *The arcade and triforium storeys of the nave of Holyrood Abbey church, and the interior of the west front. It can be seen that there were intermediate springings for the sexpartite vaulting in the middle of the bays. The plate tracery of the triforium stage, in which simple openings are cut through a flat plate of stone is also visible (the arches were originally open).*

42 (Below) *One of the capitals of the south nave arcade at Holyrood Abbey church. They are decorated with stiff-leaf foliage, in which each leaf has three curved parts.*

designed to tie in with the stone vault that covered the high central space. This vault was of the type known as sexpartite, since it had an additional intersection in the middle of each bay.

In all of this Holyrood took many ideas from Lincoln, and it may also have been from there that the inspiration was drawn for some of the more spiritedly-carved stiff-leaf foliage of the main arcade capitals and of the wall arcading in the south aisle (**42**). But by this time masons working in Scotland were beginning to have their own ideas about design as well, and the arcade piers themselves were much more massive than at

three-storeyed design which may have been modified as work progressed, but which has also been confused by later alterations (**43**). The triforium stage was no more than a series of circular openings within rather angular low arched recesses, while the small arcade which ran in front of the clearstorey passage had five arches in the bay next to the presbytery, but three in the other bays. One of the noblest parts of the design was the gable wall of the south transept, which had two tiers of finely-detailed lancets.

Kilwinning, where earlier work was incorporated along the south side of the nave, was a little larger and more complex than Dryburgh (**44**). It was evidently built to a full three-storeyed design, though the clearstorey is almost completely lost. The plan of its eastern parts was a variant on the type that is

43 *The east side of the north transept at Dryburgh Abbey church.*

Lincoln, having a stepped plan with three-quarter shafts in the angles and on the leading faces. These piers were to be followed in a number of other thirteenth-century churches, including the cathedrals of Dunblane and Glasgow.

Dryburgh, Paisley and Kilwinning

Among other major continuing campaigns at this period were those at Dryburgh, Kilwinning and Paisley Abbeys. Dryburgh had probably been laid out in the last years of the twelfth century to a plan that was a modified version of that at St Andrews and Arbroath, but in which the unaisled presbytery was relatively long while the aisled section of the choir was of only two bays. Most of what is now seen is of the early thirteenth century, however, and is of an elegant

44 *The south transept of Kilwinning Abbey church.*

particularly associated with the Cistercians. However, it had three towers, with the terminal bays of the nave opening into those at the west end in a way that almost created a second transept. In this there may have been some similarities with the sister Tironensian house of Arbroath. There the arches of the gallery and clearstorey stages were simply carried across the sides of the towers towards the nave as a screen, with no vaults separating aisle and gallery; but at Kilwinning that screen was altogether omitted.

Paisley is the most complete of this group of churches, and is still in use as a parish church, though it was extensively altered in the later Middle Ages. The most complete thirteenth-century parts are the arcade of the chapel off the south transept, the south aisle wall, the west front, parts of the western arcade piers, and the doorway into the north

aisle. All of these belong to a major campaign to build a nave with a three-storeyed internal design, and with an imposing twin-towered west front, though those towers seem never to have been built (45).

Even without its towers, and with three enormous traceried windows cut through its masonry in the later fourteenth and fifteenth centuries, the west front is still imposing, with a multiple-shafted doorway at its base which is related to that at Dunblane Cathedral. Other details, including the stiff-leaf foliage of the north doorway, are perhaps closer in spirit to the work in progress in the choir at Glasgow Cathedral around the same time. One feature of the south aisle wall which may be worth mentioning at this stage is the design of some of the windows, in which three pointed lights (individual openings) are grouped within a single arch. In such windows, as also in the triforium stage at Holyrood, we see the interest in the grouping of openings that was a prerequisite of the development of window tracery.

Some smaller-scale campaigns of the earlier thirteenth century

The Cistercians were still building actively in the earlier thirteenth century, and their approach to planning continued to influence the other orders. It may even have been one factor behind the design at Iona, where the church started soon after 1200 had an aisleless cruciform plan, with a pair of chapels on the east face of each transept. But in the north transept, which is the only survivor of this campaign, the chapels are unusually shallow, being little more than excavations into a thick wall. In the absence of much of the original abbey church at Iona, the details of the contemporary nearby Augustinian nunnery provide a guide to what was architecturally possible in the Western Isles at that time (46). The round arcade arches, and narrow splayed windows linked by prominent

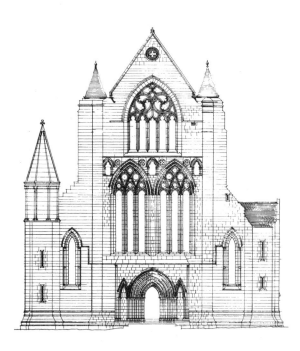

45 *The west front of Paisley Abbey church. The three large traceried windows are later insertions (National Art Survey).*

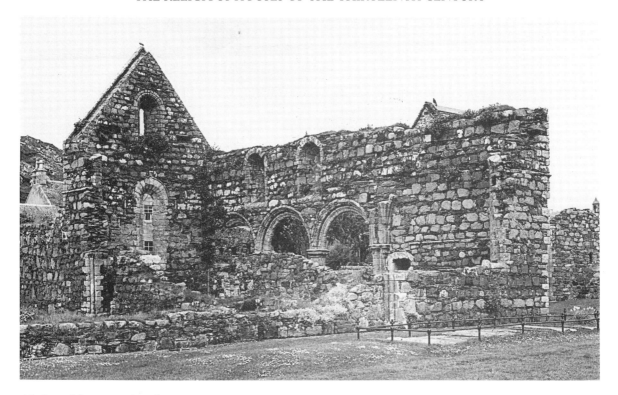

46 *Iona Nunnery church.*

string-courses, present a still essentially Romanesque approach to design that owes as much to Ireland as to Lowland Scotland. The founder of both the abbey and nunnery at Iona, Reginald, son of Somerled, variously styled 'King' or 'Lord' of the Isles, also founded the only Cistercian abbey in the Western Highlands, at Saddell. That had an even simpler plan than Iona, with the square transepts apparently being a later addition.

Much further east, two Cistercian abbeys were built in Fife, at Balmerino and Culross. Balmerino, where there are only very slight remains of the church, was probably started soon after its foundation in about 1227 by the dowager Queen Ermengarde and her son Alexander II. Its plan was almost a mirror image of that already seen at the Augustinian abbey of Cambuskenneth, being cruciform, with two chapels on each transept and a single aisle against the nave. But in this case

47 *Culross Abbey church. The original presbytery was at the far east end, and on each side are the arches leading into the transepts.*

the aisle was on the south side, presumably because the cloister was on the north, and again there are all the signs that it was an addition.

Culross was slightly earlier than Balmerino, having been founded by the Earl of Fife at a date after 1214 (47). Its plan was essentially like that at Balmerino before the addition of the aisle. However, Culross has the distinction that its eastern parts remain in use, and it has an added interest because the western of the two screens that separated the choir of the monks from that of the lay-brethren was preserved when a tower was built above it in the later Middle Ages (48). Another example of the screens which might close off the monks' choir from the rest of the church is to be seen at Inchcolm (49). In this case the screens were built along with the tower that was raised over the original choir in the early years of the thirteenth

48 *The lower part of the tower of Culross Abbey church. At its base is the screen between the two choirs, with doorways on each side of the site of the altar. When the tower was built these doorways had to be blocked, and a reused doorway was instead placed at the centre.*

49 (Right) *The tower of Inchcolm Abbey church. Within the two arches at the base of the tower were subordinate arches which formed part of the screens dividing the canons' choir and the nave; on the east side were three arches (seen here) and on the west there were two.*

century. The church was extended further eastwards later in the thirteenth century, when Bishop Richard of Dunkeld built a new choir in 1265.

One other island site where a monastic church was under construction around this period was Inchmahome, on the Lake of Menteith, which was founded by the Earl of Menteith in about 1238 (50 and **colour plate 12**). It is a small church, having an aisle-less rectangular choir (with a sacristy on its north side), a nave with an aisle on its north side, and a squat tower over the west bay of the aisle. There seem to have been changes in the course of construction, but it is essentially a homogeneous construction. The finest features are the east window, with five tall lights within a single arch, and the west front, which has a deeply recessed doorway flanked by blind arcading (51).

Inchcolm and Inchmahome were both Augustinian houses, and reference must also be made to another house of the order, at Restenneth (52). There, an aisle-less choir, with a northern sacristy, and an aisle-less nave were built to each side of the eleventh- and twelfth-century tower in two separate thirteenth-century phases. The nave is reduced to its lower walls, but the shell of the choir is almost complete. Its rhythm of single lancet-shaped windows separated by buttresses along the side walls is simple but effective, while the east wall is pierced by three single lights. An unusual feature of the church is the way the tower is off-centre to both the nave and choir, but this would not have been internally obvious when there were screens – probably of timber – to either

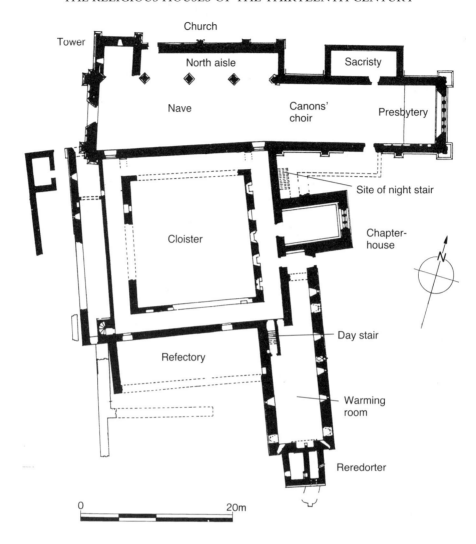

50 *The plan of Inchmahome Priory.*

side, with the nave altar being placed in the middle.

Since the original church at Inchcolm was so small, it is hardly surprising that periodic extensions should have taken place there. But monastic communities were prepared to face the upset to their lives and religious routine by undertaking expensive and disruptive rebuilding operations even when the existing buildings must have been quite commodious. At Dunfermline, for example, works were carried out in the mid-thirteenth century which slightly extended and squared-off the presbytery, and also provided a low chapel at the east end for the newly canonized St Margaret. This presumably gave the monks a little extra space for their choir and provided an access route for pilgrims to a more suitably-housed shrine, to which St Margaret's body was transferred in 1250 (**53**). Of all of this, only the lower walls of part of the shrine chapel remain, but these indicate a sophisticated design divided into bays by wall shafts, and with decorative arcading around the lower walls, which may have been rather like the aisles of the choir at Carlisle Cathedral.

51 (Above) *Interior of Inchmahome Priory church.*

52 *Restenneth Priory church. The choir is to the right of the tower.*

53 *A reconstruction sketch of the shrine chapel of St Margaret at Dunfermline Abbey.*

The churches of the Valliscaulians

The three priories founded for the Valliscaulians at Ardchattan, Beauly and Pluscarden, in or soon after 1230, represent a particularly interesting minor episode of Scottish monastic history. Substantial parts of all three churches survive, though there is little sense of any family relationship in their architecture. At Ardchattan, in Argyll, the most complete parts of the original church are portions of the south transept, and of the north and west walls of the nave. These show it was an aisle-less cruciform structure, with a pair of shallow chapels on the east face of each transept.

Beauly, in Inverness-shire, which still stands almost complete to the wall-heads, apart from a chapel added against its north side, may have started as an elongated rectangular structure, with a sacristy on its north side (54). Eventually it had a basically cross-shaped plan, though this may have

happened as a result of part of the range on the east side of the cloister – on the opposite side of the church from the sacristy – coming to be treated as a chapel. Many of the details of Beauly are well-contrived, with the windows of the choir being incorporated internally into continuous wall arcades (55). But much of this is likely to date from rather later in the century, and there were also further modifications towards the end of the Middle Ages.

The most ambitious of the Valliscaulian churches was that at Pluscarden in Moray, the surviving choir and transepts of which are now used by a Benedictine community (56). The plan is basically on the Cistercian model, and with a single south aisle on the side of the nave towards the cloister. The nave and transepts were probably started before the presbytery, suggesting that a temporary oratory was used by the monks before the new eastern limb could be built. Little remains of the nave other than part of

54 The plan of Beauly Priory church.

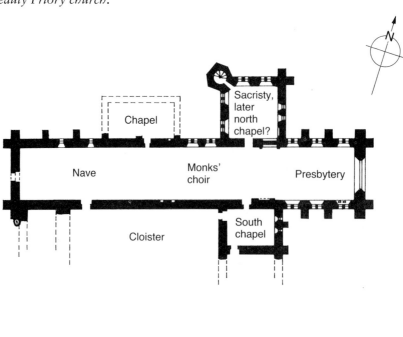

the south aisle wall, which incorporates a handsome doorway; there is also the beginning of the south arcade, in which the piers rose from a low wall against which the choir stalls would have been placed.

Construction of the transepts at Pluscarden took some years to complete, because there were several changes of design, but in both the design is for two storeys. Above the arcades is a pair of lofty arches at clearstorey level of each bay in the north transept, corresponding to the windows in the outer wall. In each bay of the south transept is a wide central arch flanked on each side by a lower

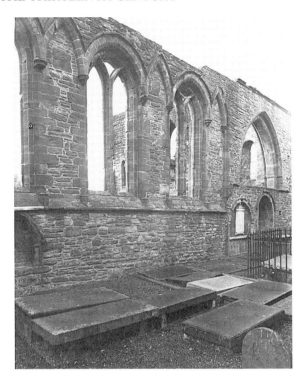

55 (Right) *The interior of the choir of Beauly Priory church, looking towards the south wall.*

56 (Below) *Pluscarden Priory from the north-east, before the recent restoration of the choir.*

arch, with the central arch corresponding to three-light clearstorey windows in the outer wall. In such designs a separate middle storey is avoided by setting the mural passage well below the level of the higher windows, the two levels being embraced by a single series of arches.

The later decades of the century

Building of the eastern limb at Pluscarden almost certainly takes us into the third quarter of the century. It was a work of considerable finesse, showing some similarities with the rebuilding started at nearby Elgin Cathedral around 1270. Carefully designed buttresses define the bays and angles, and vast windows extended to fill nearly all of the space between those buttresses. But the most remarkable features were the tracery of the windows and the stone vaulting over the whole of the eastern limb; other than over aisles, vaulting continued to be a rare extravagance at this time.

Both of these features are now lost, the vaulting having been later replaced by a timber ceiling and the windows by much smaller ones. Nevertheless, it is still possible to understand what was once there. The windows were filled with what is known as bar tracery, because of the way the patterns are created by curved stone bars of uniform section rather than being cut through thin plates of stone as in the earlier type of tracery. Such tracery had been developed in France from the early decades of the century, and was probably introduced into England at the royal work of Westminster Abbey in the 1240s. The earliest datable examples in Scotland are of around the 1260s and 1270s, as for example at Glasgow and Elgin Cathedrals. At Pluscarden the windows must have been divided into two sub-groups of two lights each, within containing arches which had a circlet at their head; a third and larger circlet was placed between the two

containing arches and the main window arch.

Another impressive group of tracery was also being created around this time in the far south-west of the country, at the Cistercian abbey church of Sweetheart, founded by Devorguilla Balliol in 1273 (57). Despite being the last new house of the order in Scotland, and although the churches at Newbattle and Kinloss had already been given more complex plans, Sweetheart was still set out to the traditional Cistercian plan – although, as we have seen, such plans were no longer limited to the order. Something of the earlier Cistercian spirit is again evident in the relatively simple two-storeyed design of the transepts and nave, with three openings at clearstorey level in each bay. The same is also true of the squat crossing tower, which rose only a little above the roofs that converged on its four sides. But an altogether more modern spirit was demonstrated in the form of the nave arcade piers, which show a new and more plastically-modelled development on the bundled-shaft piers seen in churches of around a century earlier.

This more modern spirit is even more evident in the design of the windows of the presbytery and transepts (58). The most impressive of them is that in the east gable, which is an expansion of the design type seen at Pluscarden, with an additional light between the two grouped pairs. Among the designs in the flanks of the presbytery was a more advanced type, with a scattering of three circlets around the heads of the three lights. A puzzling feature of these windows, however, is that some seem to have been designed from the start to have the glass set directly into narrow chases in the stonework, while in others it appears it was intended the glass should be in timber frames, as had been usual earlier.

The last building to be mentioned here is the freestanding bell tower at Cambuskenneth, which is the one part of the complex

57 *The interior of Sweetheart Abbey church,*
looking eastwards.

58 (Above) *The south flank of the presbytery of Sweetheart Abbey church. The windows are filled with bar tracery, in which the individual forms are defined by curved bars of stone.*

59 (Right) *The bell tower of Cambuskenneth Abbey; in the foreground are the foundations of the nave and transept of the abbey church.*

there that still stands to full height (**59** and **colour plate 5**). It is possible there may be earlier work at the lower levels, but most of what is now seen can probably be dated to the later decades of the thirteenth century. It rises through three main storeys, with a stair turret at its north-east corner. The bold profile and high quality detailing of the tower are probably because it was designed to be seen from the royal castle of Stirling, on its rock to the west, and it is still an important landmark in the view from there.

CHAPTER SIX

The Fourteenth and Earlier Fifteenth Centuries

The historical background

The fourteenth century was a time of mixed fortunes for Scotland and its church. The death of Alexander III in 1286, followed in 1290 by that of his granddaughter and only direct heiress, the Maid of Norway, had left Scotland with no undisputed claimant to the throne. Edward I of England's adjudication in favour of John Balliol in 1292 brought only a temporary solution and, when the Scots refused to be as pliant to Edward's wishes as he required, in 1296 he marched north on a punitive expedition, deposing John in the process. Nearly two decades of debilitating war followed, until Robert I's re-establishment of independence following Bannockburn in 1314 and the recapture of Berwick in 1318 led to a renewed sense of national identity. The high-point was in 1328, when both the English and the pope recognized Scotland's sovereignty.

This, however, was followed a year later by Robert I's death, the succession of the infant David II and the opening of a new phase of warfare with England. David was eventually able to return from France in 1341, where he had been sent for his own safe-keeping, but was captured by the English five years later at the battle of Neville's Cross, and was in captivity for a further eleven years. Following his return, Scotland entered a new period of relative prosperity, and a

fourteen-year truce with England was confirmed in 1369, which seems generally to have held. But it was highly objectionable to the Scots that English forces continued to hold parts of southern Scotland, and the recapture of some of these in 1385 led to a new phase of periodic warfare, in which the Border abbeys suffered particularly badly. A new low point was reached in 1406, when the future James I was captured by the English on his way to France, supposedly for the benefit of his education, but perhaps also to escape the attentions of his uncle, the Duke of Albany, in whose custody his oldest brother had already died. James was not eventually released until 1424.

The effects of long years of intermittent warfare with England meant that – with some notable exceptions – there were few occasions when resources could be found for expensive building operations at the existing religious houses during the greater part of the fourteenth century. This same factor, coupled with the generally lower esteem in which the religious orders had come to be held, also meant that very few new foundations were made for them throughout the whole of the fourteenth century. Small priories of Augustinians were set up at St Fillan's, Pittenweem and Oronsay, and there was a new house for the Trinitarians at Fail. Otherwise the only new foundations were for the mendicant orders: for the

Franciscans at Lanark, the Dominicans at Cupar and the Carmelites at Banff. Things did not improve greatly before the middle of the fifteenth century. Other than a Carmelite nunnery at Linlithgow, the only important foundation of the early decades of the century was the handsomely-endowed Charterhouse which James I founded on the outskirts of Perth, and of which nothing now remains.

The breakdown of relations with England also had a far-reaching impact on architectural developments in Scotland. In England the last years of the thirteenth and first decades of the fourteenth centuries were a particularly creative period, and for a while the work produced by masons there was perhaps in advance of anything elsewhere in Europe. Two seemingly opposed and yet interlinked strands of thought predominated in England. On the one hand, the freedoms encouraged by the double-curved ogee motif resulted in sinuously flowing tracery forms of the 'Decorated' style, which were eventually to be taken up with even greater enthusiasm elsewhere in Europe. On the other hand, an ultimately French-inspired approach to emphatically horizontal and vertical articulation of wall faces and window tracery led to a taste for emphasized rectilinearity, which was to set the pattern for the uniquely English 'Perpendicular' style of the later Middle Ages.

However, because there were relatively so few opportunities for building at this time, Scotland played very little part in these developments, and when major church building operations began again, towards the end of the fourteenth century, there is apparent a growing reluctance to re-establish the links that had previously existed with England. Not only was England now firmly established as the enemy, but architecture there had recently undergone a period of rapid change and must have come to look distinctly alien. Beyond that, in the interim Scotland had established strong political, commercial, intellectual and cultural links with other parts of Europe – most notably with France and the Low Countries – and to many of Scotland's potential patrons the architecture of those countries must have looked no more unfamiliar than that of England. As a result of new influences coming from those countries, we find – perversely enough – an emerging approach to architectural design in which there was a blending of ideas that was perhaps more distinctly Scottish than at any other period. We have lost so many important buildings that we cannot hope to understand fully all of the ideas that lay behind this synthesis, but from a number of monastic churches we can at least gain some idea.

Monastic churches before the later part of the century

The most splendid structures to be raised for any of the religious orders in the earlier fourteenth century were the refectory and guest house at Dunfermline, but these will be dealt with later, as part of the survey of monastic buildings. The few monastic churches that we know of from this period are rather less inspiring. At the small Augustinian priory of St Fillan's, in Glendochart, which originated in a grant of Robert I in 1317-18 to an existing church, and to which gifts were being made in 1329, there is little other than rather enigmatic remains which may have been part of the church.

Of a partly similar date, but rather more complete, are the remains of the Augustinian priory on the island of Oronsay. This is said to have been founded by the first of the Lords of the Isles named John, which would place it after 1325, and there is a reference to a prior in 1358. The church, which was originally a basically rectangular unaisled structure, has been modified on a number of occasions. However, although it is notoriously difficult to date structures built of rubble masonry and with few original architectural features, there seems little reason to date it long after the foundation.

The finest monastic church of the early and mid-fourteenth century is that of the Premonstratensian priory of Fearn, in Easter Ross, which is still in use as a parish church (**60**). It had been founded in the 1220s, but the church is said to have been rebuilt by Abbot Mark after about 1338, and to have been completed by Abbot Donald in 1372. Its western parts have been truncated and a number of lateral aisles have been added around its periphery, but it was originally of simple rectangular plan. The best detailing is in the presbytery area, which is strengthened by broadly-projecting buttresses and lit by lancet windows that rest upon a continuous string-course. The east wall has an impressive grouping of four equal-height lancets.

60 Fearn Abbey church, from the south-east.

St Andrews

If the early and mid-fourteenth centuries were generally a rather low point for monastic churches, the later decades of the century saw the beginning of a revival that produced several highly significant buildings. Apart from a number of lesser operations on existing churches such as Sweetheart, Dryburgh and Pluscarden, the most important about which anything is known were at St Andrews, Melrose and Paisley.

The work at St Andrews was necessitated by a fire in 1378 and, while rebuilding was still in progress, there was a further calamity when the south transept gable collapsed in 1409. The chief surviving evidence for rebuilding in the nave is seen in a number of the arcade pier bases, and in the upper parts of the west front. The pier bases are elongated towards the central space in a way which points to a sophisticated division into bays by wall shafts rising the full height of

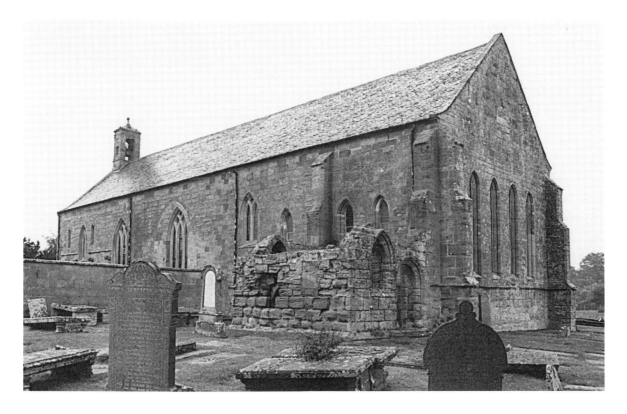

the elevation. On the west front the most interesting feature is the tracery of the main windows, which was apparently in the form of a triangular arrangement of three circlets (**61**). This was a type of tracery that had been first developed in France around the 1230s, but soon afterwards taken up elsewhere, and we have already mentioned a variant of the idea at Sweetheart.

However, at St Andrews it may be significant that the area of tracery was lifted up above the arched heads of the lights in a way that is described as stilting. Since this is something that is more frequently a feature of French than of English window design, could it be that there was French influence behind the design of the new work at St Andrews? In this connection it is worth remembering that as early as 1329 Robert I's tomb for Dunfermline had been commissioned in Paris, so it would be nothing new by this stage to look to France. Beyond that, of the two bishops who are most likely to have been in charge at the time the work was carried out, both had French connections. Bishop William Landallis (1342–85) had been elected to the diocese with the support of Philip VI of France, and Bishop Walter Trail (1385-1401) had been a student at the universities of Paris and Orleans. Of course, on such limited evidence French influence can only be one possible explanation for aspects of the design of St Andrews, but we shall consider this possibility further after looking at Melrose.

Melrose and Paisley

The complexities of the architectural situation at this time are nowhere more obvious than at Melrose (**62** and **colour plate 7**). Rebuilding there was necessitated by an English attack in 1385, in the time of Richard II. When rebuilding was started it was almost certainly under the aegis of the English king, who made provision for the

61 *The west front of St Andrews cathedral church. The window above the great doorway can be seen probably to have had three large circlets at its head.*

funding of the work in 1389, and who probably regarded southern Scotland as having been reconquered. In plan the new church was laid out as a larger version of what was already there, a variant on the Cistercian plan in which the transept chapels next to the presbytery step a little further east than the others. The first phase of rebuilding encompassed the main structure of the presbytery and south transept, and the eastern parts of the shell of the north transept; the arcades of the three eastern bays of the nave were probably also started, since this was the part that housed the choir of the monks.

The quality of the new work is outstandingly high, and it is lavishly enriched with sculptural decoration. The most obvious pointer to an English mason being behind the design is the window tracery of the earliest parts, in which there is the influence of the English 'Perpendicular' style in the combination of verticals rising through the full height of the windows and the frequent horizontal transoms. Even more significantly, the rather hard angularity, which is seen particularly in the east window, points to an eastern English origin for the mason. A related approach to window design is to be seen in a number of churches in both East Anglia and the East Riding of Yorkshire, including King's Lynn St Nicholas in Norfolk and Beverley St Mary in Yorkshire. But Yorkshire may be a more likely place of origin for the mason, since the way the eastern gable and the buttresses which flank it are enriched by a lavish display of carved niches seems to belong in the same tradition as is represented in the design of the choir gable at the collegiate church of Howden. There could also be parallels with Howden in some of the details of the two-storeyed design of the interior. It is less easy to find prototypes for the rather tunnel-like vault over the choir, with its net-like patterning of ribs, though this was perhaps ultimately inspired by examples in the west of England.

62 Melrose Abbey church from the south-east. The window tracery of the presbytery, to the right of this view, reflects the rectilinearity of English 'Perpendicular' works.

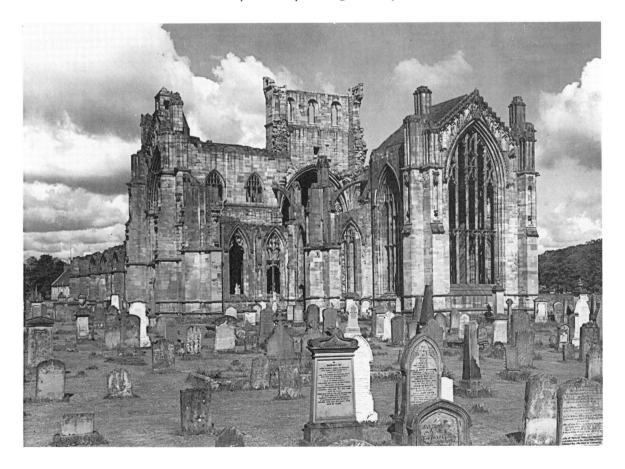

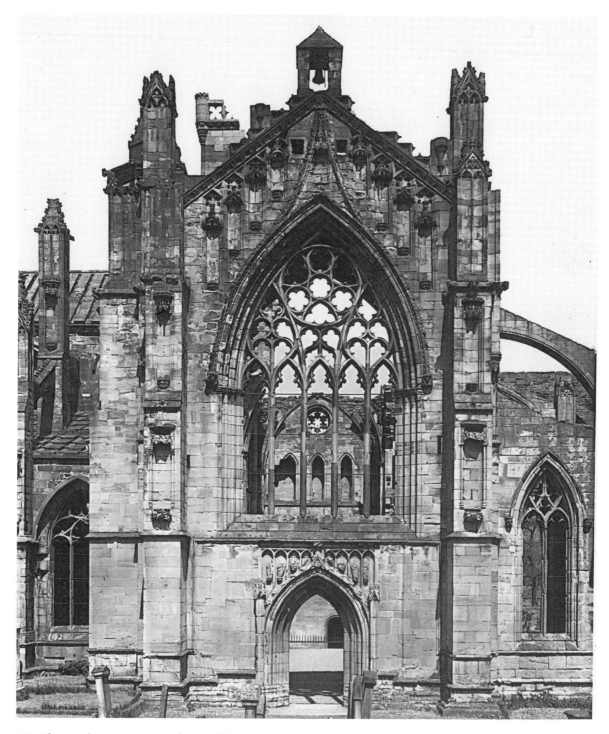

63 *The south transept at Melrose Abbey church.*
Although its basic design is similar to that of the
presbytery gable, its flowing tracery design is very
different.

In all of this, the first parts of Melrose are unquestionably English, and it might be assumed from this that Scotland was once again to build up its relationship with architecture south of the Border. But these English details were to be reflected in very few other buildings, and it is at Melrose itself that we see one of the clearest pointers to the change that was coming about in Scottish architecture. In a number of windows in the presbytery and transepts, and also in the earliest windows of a row of chapels added against the south flank of the nave, we see a dramatic change in the tracery design (63). Instead of the rectilinearity of the first windows we find compositions in which curvilinear forms predominate. Such complex flowing forms had been first developed in England in the years after 1300, and it might therefore be argued that in this second phase tracery at Melrose we see designs looking back to an earlier phase of English architecture. But tracery like this had also been taken up and developed in other parts of Europe, after it had been abandoned in England. There is thus the alternative possibility that, by the early years of the fifteenth century, Melrose was looking to continental Europe rather than England for inspiration, as it has earlier been suggested was the case in the windows of the west front of St Andrews Cathedral.

Fortunately, at Melrose we know that it is this second possibility that is the more likely, since a French-born mason inserted two inscriptions in the south transept with a lack of modesty for which we must be eternally grateful. These proclaim that a mason named John Morow was at work here, and that he had been born in Paris. It may also have been the idea of this same mason that the outer row of chapels should be added on the side of the nave away from the cloister, since this was being done at several continental houses of the Cistercians in order to provide additional altar space. Beyond their importance for Melrose, Morow's inscriptions are invaluable for the list of other churches on which he was involved. One of these was St Andrews and, although the new west windows discussed above do not themselves look to be by Morow, this may suggest that a group of French masons had been at work there, of which Morow himself was one.

Morow's contribution can be more positively identified at a small number of the other buildings he includes in his list. Of these the most important for our purposes is Paisley Abbey. There the eastern bays of the north aisle, which probably pre-date Abbot Lithgow's choice of a burial place in the vicinity of the north porch in 1433, show the clear hallmarks of his hand. One window is not only almost identical with the first window of the outer chapels at Melrose, but has the same unusual mouldings around it. It is worth noting here that virtually the same window, within very similar mouldings, was also used at another of Morow's works, the collegiate church of Lincluden on the outskirts of Dumfries.

In what we can still see of the architecture built to the designs of Morow we find highly refined details which are probably little different from what he would have expected to produce in France – except perhaps for the scale. Towards the end of the Middle Ages we again find other examples of continental masons being allowed to build as they would in their own countries, especially in some of the royal palaces. However, more frequently ideas of foreign origin have been adapted to Scottish tastes and purses in a way which suggests they were the work of Scottish craftsmen. But, whatever the means by which these ideas reached Scotland, the results were to take its architecture along a very different path from that followed south of the Border. As the fifteenth century advanced, the monasteries were perhaps no longer so much at the forefront in developing new ideas as they once had been, but they still had an important contribution to make.

CHAPTER SEVEN

The Later Middle Ages

Patronage of the religious orders in the later Middle Ages

After a long period during which the religious orders had acquired very few new foundations, by the middle decades of the fifteenth century there was the beginning of a steady trickle of fresh activity, and this was to continue into the first quarter of the sixteenth century. However, disenchantment with the growing worldliness of the older orders, together with what may have been a recognition that saturation point had been reached so far as they were concerned, meant that nearly all new foundations were for the more recent forms of religious life. Apart from the exceptional foundation for the Carthusians in Perth by James I in 1429 and a rather enigmatic house for Cistercian nuns at St Evoca in Kirkcudbrightshire, they were all for the friars or the orders of nuns attached to them. It also seems it was the more up-to-date forms of mendicancy that were especially favoured since, apart from a single foundation for the Conventual Franciscans at Kirkcudbright in the mid-fifteenth century, all of the nine other houses established for the order were for their more austere Observant branch.

Yet, despite the lack of new foundations for the older orders, many of the existing houses were still very wealthy and were able to build on the grand scale if they so wished.

Several abbeys wholly or partly rebuilt their churches or monastic buildings, and there are few of which anything remains where there is not evidence of some late medieval rebuilding. Sometimes this rebuilding was necessitated by damage resulting from warfare or hostile action, while on other occasions it followed structural collapse. But in many cases it must have been simply in response to a wish for more commodious or more fashionable buildings. Of the houses of the older orders, surviving buildings tell of major church reconstruction operations in the course of the fifteenth and sixteenth centuries at Crossraguel, Inchcolm, Iona, Melrose and Paisley. We must also assume there were others where the evidence no longer survives. Less extensive operations were being carried out at Ardchattan, Beauly, Culross, Dryburgh, Dunfermline, Holyrood, Jedburgh, Peebles, Restenneth, Tongland and Torphichen. All of this shows that the older houses were still capable of considerable energy, even if their spiritual standards were less exacting than they had been.

There must also have been much activity in the mendicant houses, and there are still major remains of the churches of the Carmelites at South Queensferry, of the Observant Franciscans at Elgin and of the church granted to the Dominicans at St Monans. We also have significant remains of the Dominican church at St Andrews and of the Carmelite church at Luffness, while at least something is known of the Observant churches at Aberdeen and Jedburgh, and of the Carmelite churches at Aberdeen, Linlithgow and Perth.

Inchcolm and South Queensferry

Two churches under construction in the first half of the fifteenth century were those of the Augustinians on Inchcolm and of the Carmelites at South Queensferry. In them we see emerging a particularly Scottish approach to small-scale church design, which had much in common with castle construction.

At Inchcolm the unusual decision was taken to build a completely new church to the east of the existing structure and, apart from the bell tower, the original church was eventually put to other uses or demolished (64). It was set out to an aisle-less plan that was closer to a Greek than a Latin cross, the main space continuing past the transeptal chapels with no break other than the arches opening into them. The continuity of this space was apparently emphasized by being covered by a single barrel vault of pointed section (65). Similar vaults were placed over

64 *The plan of Inchcolm Abbey.*

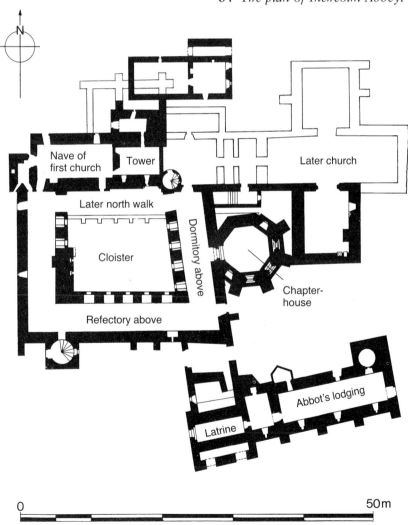

65 *Inchcolm Abbey church from the east. The lower walls of the presbytery and of the north transept of the later church are in the foreground, and the vault springing of its south transept is on the left. The pyramidal chapter-house roof and the tower of the earlier church are behind.*

the transeptal chapels, part of the southern one of which still survives. Although vaults of this type had been used in a number of castles, this may have been one of the first occasions it was used in a church. It was, however, soon to be copied in several others.

A reason for the use of these vaults at Inchcolm was perhaps that the abbey was on a vulnerable site in the Firth of Forth, and had been attacked several times. It was probably the strong and fireproof construction that was so attractive. The date of the new church at Inchcolm is uncertain, though the

south chapel is thought to have been the Lady Chapel, and there is a record that this was under construction in 1402 under the direction of Prior Richard of Aberdour and Canon Thomas Crawford.

Most of Inchcolm church has been lost, but something of its architectural qualities can still be understood from the Carmelite church at South Queensferry which was founded in 1440 by James Dundas of Dundas (**66**). At Queensferry there was a central tower and a single south transeptal chapel on the side away from the cloister, and so there was greater compartmentalization of the spaces than at Inchcolm. Yet the scale of those spaces, and the way they are covered by pointed barrel vaults, is very similar. In such churches there is a predominant sense of wall surface, since it extends up into the curved faces of the vault without break; additionally, the windows tend to be low-set

66 *The vaulted choir of the Carmelite Friary church at South Queensferry.*

Paisley and Crossraguel

The diversity of approach at this period of architectural experimentation is nowhere more evident than in the two church building operations under way around the central decades of the fifteenth century for the Cluniac order. The more ambitious of the two was in the nave of Paisley, where a new central space was created within the outer envelope that had been constructed at various times during the thirteenth, fourteenth and early fifteenth centuries (67). This was the work of Abbot Thomas Tervas (1445–59), and was perhaps complete by the time he imported a magnificent altarpiece in 1455. In fact Tervas's mason was severely limited by what had already been built, and the result was a rather conservative three-storeyed design in which paired openings within the limits of a single containing arch at triforium level corresponded to pairs of windows at clearstorey level. The most striking feature of the design was the way

to keep them below the level of the vault. Nevertheless, the slightly ponderous appearance of weight created by the bare stone walls as now seen would originally have been less severe, since they would have been plastered and painted.

67 *A cross-section of the Abbey church at Paisley before restoration (National Art Survey).*

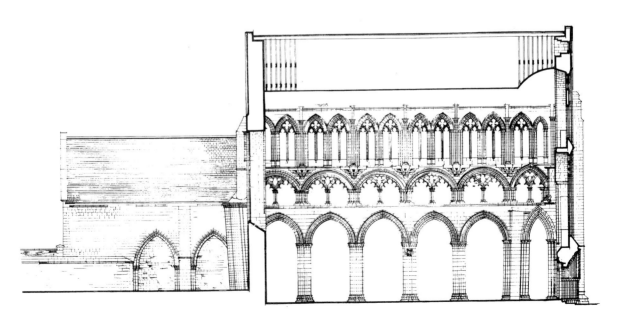

the clearstorey passage was carried around the principal piers at that level on massive three-tiered corbels. The slightly ungainly appearance of these corbels would have been mitigated when they carried the balustrade intended for them. In this treatment we perhaps see distant echoes of European prototypes such as the corbelled-out galleries in the aisles of St Lorenz at Nürnberg.

Crossraguel was much poorer than its mother house at Paisley, and yet the new choir built for it was more architecturally innovative (**68** and **colour plate 6**). According to a tradition recorded in the early

68 Crossraguel Abbey, looking across from the site of the abbot's house to the choir and presbytery of the church. At the centre is the two-storeyed range which contained the chapter-house, sacristy and dormitory.

eighteenth century, this work was carried out for Abbot Colin (1460–91). The new choir was a five-bay single-storeyed aisle-less space of only modest scale, but its architectural details were notably fine and at its east end was a polygonal apse as the setting for the high altar. Such apses were one of the clearest pointers to European inspiration in Scottish architecture at this time, since they were the norm on the Continent but rare in England. The earliest of them may have been that which Bishop Kennedy of St Andrews built for his collegiate chapel of St Salvator between 1450 and 1460, and it is possible Crossraguel was inspired directly by that example, particularly since Kennedy was of an Ayrshire family.

Externally the design is dominated by the large windows, which fill most of the available space between the buttresses, and it is unfortunate that none of the tracery remains to help us understand the sources of the

69 *Iona Abbey church, from the south-east, before restoration. The presbytery is to the right and the south transept to the left (R.W. Billings).*

design more fully. Internally an unusual feature is the slight outward projection above a roll moulding of the upper wall at the level of the window arches. There are also some excellent furnishings, including the canopied *piscina*, where the vessels used at the mass were washed, and the recessed seats known as the *sedilia* where the clergy sat for part of the services. Permanent fixtures and furnishings were becoming an increasingly important element of church design at this period. Of the various other church building operations under way for the religious orders at this time, only the continuing work at

Melrose seems to have surpassed Crossraguel in quality, and there are several fine *piscinae* in the chapels there.

Iona

All of the buildings so far discussed in this chapter are in the Lowland areas, where the great majority of Scotland's religious houses were concentrated. But there were also several campaigns of reconstruction at monastic churches in the Highlands at this period. Valliscaulian Ardchattan provided itself with a larger rectangular eastern limb, for example, and there was probably also work on the Augustinian church at Oronsay. However, undoubtedly the most prestigious campaign was at Iona (**69**). Work here was probably carried out for the energetic Abbot Dominic

(1421–*c*.65), who rescued the abbey's finances from earlier mismanagement at the hands of the MacKinnon clan.

Much of what is now seen at Iona is a result of modern restoration, but the eastern limb and south transept are still essentially as remodelled in the later Middle Ages. As the main elements of this operation a crypt was suppressed and the choir and presbytery floor level lowered, the eastern bay of the presbytery was rebuilt, the north aisle was truncated to form a sacristy block, and the south choir aisle and south transept were largely rebuilt, together with a squat tower over the crossing. The most 'architectural' features of this work, including the window tracery and the cylindrical columns of the south aisle, show an awareness of ideas that were current in the Lowland areas. Yet there is a difference of approach which must result from the nearness to Ireland, and the employment of at least one mason of Irish origin is attested by an inscription on the south arcade. Again we are reminded that it could be easier to reach the Western Highlands from Ireland than from Lowland Scotland. However, that is not to say that Iona looks like an Irish building of the same period, but rather to suggest that there were other factors at work here than operated in the Lowlands, with fascinating consequences for the architecture.

70 *Jedburgh Abbey church from the north. The extended north transept is to the left.*

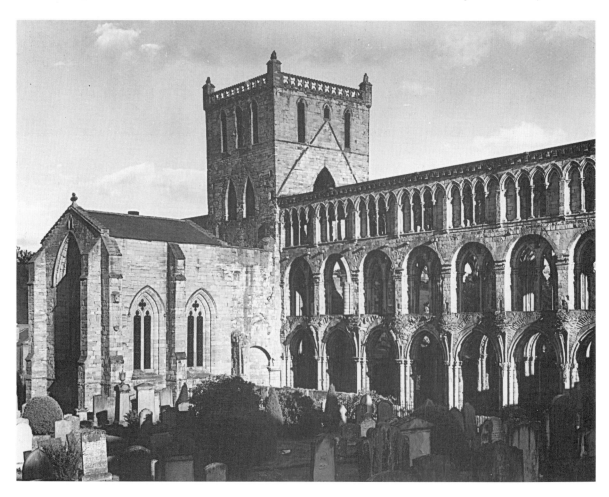

Enlarged transepts

In rebuilding Iona the south transept was given a different form from its northern counterpart, of soon after 1200. In fact this new transept was very much less asymmetrical than a large unfinished predecessor of the thirteenth century would have been, but it is a significant pointer to the attitudes of the period that it was not felt inappropriate for even major churches to be asymmetrically planned to each side of the main east–west axis. We have already noted that South Queensferry had a single transept and, while most major churches still tended to have two, there was no sense of inconsistency in giving them different designs.

The principal reason for the enlargement of transepts may well have been to provide additional space for altars at a time when there was a growing demand for prayers to be said for the souls of the dead. At Jedburgh Abbey, for example, the north transept was greatly enlarged, and was provided with a tomb recess below the main window in the gable end; along with this was a blank eastern wall against which altar retables could be placed, with windows in the west wall to cast light on to those altars (70). It seems it was intended to cover Jedburgh's enlarged transept with a pointed vault like those at South Queensferry, although the scale and height of the transept led to second thoughts. The date of the transept is indicated by arms on the north wall thought to be of Bishop William Turnbull of Glasgow (1447–54), and this is supported by the similarity of the window in the north wall to one at Melrose attributable to Abbot Andrew Hunter (1441–71).

In these cases the absence of a completely symmetrical arrangement must have been masked by the way in which one of the transepts acted as a transitional element between the crossing area of the church and the range on the east side of the cloister. The

71 *The transepts of Torphichen preceptory church, looking southwards. A tomb recess may be seen beneath the window.*

enlarged transept was naturally that on the side away from the cloister. This is also the case at the Hospitaller church of Torphichen where, around the 1430s, in the time of Preceptor Andrew Meldrum, the transepts and crossing area were largely rebuilt, with a fine ribbed vault over them (71). As at Jedburgh, that away from the cloister, on the south, had a mainly blank east wall as the setting for an altar, and a large window in the gable wall with a tomb recess beneath. In the north transept, however, the presence of the cloister meant the window had to be in the east wall, behind the site of the altar. Two further elements which show how architectural taste was developing at this time are the continuously diagonal mouldings of the capitals and bases of the responds which carry the vaulting, and the designs of the window tracery, which are essentially revivals of later thirteenth-century types. Similar caps and bases are to be found in a number of late buildings, while it seems from the tracery that, at a time when masons were looking for fresh sources of inspiration, Scotland's own past was regarded as one such source.

Paisley was another abbey church which was given an enlarged transept on the side away from the cloister, on a comparable scale to that at Jedburgh. There the work is probably datable to the very end of the century, since it has been linked with Abbot Robert Shaw (1499–1525). Around the same period at Paisley the chapel of St Mirren, off the south transept, was adapted to a very different design. This included the addition of a stone covering of a type increasingly favoured in Scotland, with a surface application of ribs to a pointed barrel vault. The east window of this chapel has tracery which, as at Torphichen, looks back to thirteenth-century types.

Towers

Where monastic churches were deemed to be adequate to meet the needs of a community without major rebuilding, a favourite addition was a tower or spire. Several of these have survived, while we know of others from documentary records or physical evidence, like the tower added to Kinloss or the spire placed on the tower of St Rule's at St Andrews.

Among these added towers is the plain example tacked on to the west end of Crosskirk at Peebles after it became the permanent home of a community of Trinitarians, probably around the 1470s. A more impressive tower was built over the west end of the monastic choir at Cistercian Culross by Abbot Andrew Masoun (1498-1513), and which has already been referred to as the reason why the early thirteenth-

century screen there survived. One of the most elegant of the spires added to an earlier tower is to be seen at the Augustinian priory of Restenneth, despite the fact that it can hardly have been viable as a community by the time the spire was added. It is built of fine ashlar, with simple lucarnes (tall gabled windows) at the base on all four sides. It was designed to the splay-foot form that was particularly favoured in Scotland, the preference for which may be another indicator of the influence of ideas from the Low Countries.

The churches of the friars

So far, apart from the Carmelite Church at South Queensferry, little reference has been made to the churches of the orders of friars. On the limited available evidence it appears the majority of mendicant churches were relatively simple structures, and in most cases they were set out to a basically rectangular plan. There may, however, have been structural divisions between choir and nave, as has been found to be the case at the excavated Carmelite churches of Luffness and Linlithgow. Sometimes those structural divisions must have been substantial, and a view of the Dominican church at Glasgow suggests it there took the form of a walk-way enclosed by full-height walls, which supported a bell-cote on transverse arches. This arrangement was relatively common in English mendicant houses, although the only certain case in Scotland was at the Trinitarian house of Dunbar, which is rather surprising since the Trinitarians were not friars in the strict sense. At Dunbar the walk-way and the short tower it carried have survived because they were converted into a dovecot, but excavations in 1981 show that it was near the mid-point of a rectangular plan, and it is possible there was a similar arrangement at Glasgow.

In other mendicant houses the division between choir and nave was by timber screens. A modern version of such a screen is to be seen at the Observant Franciscan church of Elgin, which was founded in 1494-5, and which was restored by John Kinross for the Convent of Mercy in 1896. The nave altars were placed on each side of the central doorway of the timber screen, and there would also have been altars on the platform, known as the rood loft, which rested on top of the screen. Windows were provided in the side wall away from the cloister to light both levels. There was a similar arrangement in the more architecturally ambitious church of the Observants in Aberdeen, which was rebuilt for them by Bishop Gavin Dunbar and Canon Alexander Galloway before the former's death in 1532. Investigations at the time of the church's demolition in 1902 revealed traces of windows at the two levels and of a stair up to the platform. However, this was not a specifically mendicant arrangement, since it is also found at a number of other Scottish churches, including the collegiate churches at Foulis Easter and Innerpeffray. What we see in these cases, then, is the mendicants adopting architectural solutions that were already accepted in Scotland rather than developing forms for their own particular use.

Of the more architecturally complex churches built for the mendicants, the most complete survivor is that of the Dominicans at St Monans. But there the order was given an existing chapel that had been built by David II between 1362 and 1370, and the main alterations carried out for the Dominicans may have amounted to no more than the insertion of new windows and the construction of a stone vault. The latter is a rather curious hybrid with miniature intersections in the middle of each bay.

Apart from St Monans, the most complete fragment of a Dominican church is that at St Andrews (**72**). This was rebuilt with money that had been left by Bishop William Elphinstone of Aberdeen, which was devoted to this purpose in 1516. Construction of the single chapel, which is all that survives, may perhaps be linked with permission to encroach into the road in 1525. This chapel, which is of polygonal plan, projected from the flank of the church, and in this it shows similarities with chapels attached to the churches at Ladykirk in Berwickshire and Arbuthnott in Kincardineshire. Yet chapels like this were also to be found in continental churches and, since the window tracery in the chapel is made up of large simplified loop-like designs which were probably inspired by prototypes in the Netherlands, it is possible the idea for the chapel's plan also came from there. This possibility is supported by the fact that the Scottish Dominicans had recently been revitalized following a visitation by the Congregation of Holland. Nevertheless, there are still elements in the design that are Scottish in origin, including the blank east wall for an altar, and the barrel vault with a surface application of ribs, related to that already referred to in St Mirren's Aisle at Paisley Abbey. All of this reminds us, of course, that Scottish masons did not simply copy what they had seen elsewhere, but were well able to create an effective new blend of ideas to meet the needs of their patrons.

Reconstruction necessitated by structural failure

Returning to the churches of the older orders, in a period when building was still an essentially practical rather than theoretical process, structural failure at monastic churches was by no means an uncommon crisis. At Dunfermline there is a long-standing problem of structural settlement, probably because of the sloping site, but the most significant late medieval rebuilding took place in the time of Abbot Richard Bothwell (1446-82), when the north-east corner of the nave had to be reconstructed. Further rebuilding in the late sixteenth century has made it difficult to be certain quite what was done, but it seems work embraced the two western bays of the north aisle, together with the lower part of the north-west tower, and at the same time a porch was added over the main entrance for layfolk. It is an interesting pointer to the aesthetic attitudes of the time that, while the upper storeys of the nave were rebuilt in a simplified version of the Romanesque work, the new pier was given a completely different form. This was perhaps because the interior spaces of the nave at the lowest level were so broken up by the screens around the many altars by this time that it was felt there would be no inconsistency in such a change.

Another major abbey where structural repairs were necessary was Holyrood, where the ambitious early thirteenth-century vaulting over the high space was threatening collapse. Much of the vault must have been reconstructed in the time of abbots

Crawford (1450–c.83) and Bellenden (1484–97), and massive supporting buttresses were added along the sides of the nave. But in operations like this the opportunity was usually taken to carry out other works, and at Holyrood a more elaborate doorway was provided on the north side of the nave to give greater emphasis to the entrance for layfolk. An even more interesting survival from this period is the new screen which was built by Crawford at the east end of the north nave aisle as one of those which separated the parts of the church used by the canons from those which were more generally accessible. Such a screen is a very rare survival in Scotland, and is a welcome pointer to the design of such fixtures.

72 *The apsidal north chapel of the Dominican church at St Andrews. It can be seen that the window tracery is made up of simple loop-like forms.*

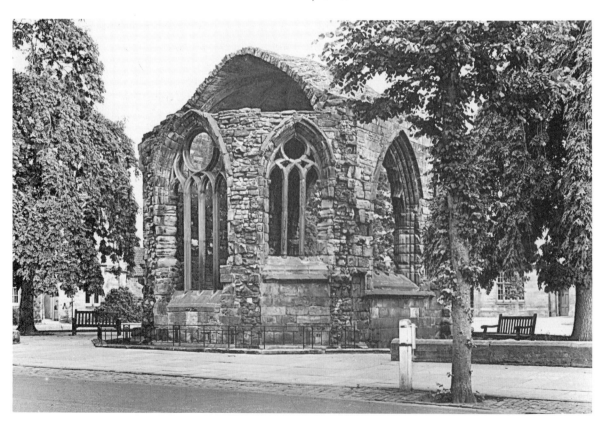

Among other works presumably occasioned by structural problems was the reconstruction of the west front at Beauly Priory, which by this time considered itself to be a Cistercian rather than a Valliscaulian house. This work was carried out by Robert Reid, who had become abbot of the house in 1531, and was later its commendator. He brought new life and vigour to the house after a period of decline. The west front he built, with a central doorway and a staggered grouping of three lancet windows at the upper level, is a modestly satisfying composition.

Reconstruction necessitated by hostile action

Hostile action was not confined to the areas near the Border since proximity to the Highlands could also be a problem at some periods. Nevertheless, the monasteries in the Borders and Lothian faced a particular problem in the later phases of the wars with England. It may have been the invasion of 1385 – that which led to the rebuilding of Melrose – which also necessitated the rebuilding of much of the nave at nearby Dryburgh. There it seems the decision was initially taken to rebuild the nave only to a reduced plan, although it was eventually fully rebuilt. Further attacks on the southern abbeys took place on several occasions in the course of the fifteenth century, but some of the most devastating damage was suffered in the course of the English incursions which followed the Scottish refusal to ratify the Treaty of Greenwich, under which it had been agreed that Mary Queen of Scots should be married to Henry VIII's son, Prince Edward. Particularly grievous damage was inflicted on several houses in 1544 and 1547. The cumulative effect of these attacks may have been one factor which resulted in Melrose never being completed as planned in the 1380s, though the sheer scale of the operation envisaged then was perhaps as much a factor.

It is at Jedburgh that we can best assess how the succession of attacks eventually took its toll. Repairs after the earlier onslaughts seem to have been initiated with great zeal, and say much for the continuing vigour of the community at those times. The work on the north transept, which has already been mentioned, may have been partly in response to English destruction in 1410 and 1416. Remodelling of the south choir chapel may also have been undertaken for the same reason, though it had to be repaired yet again, perhaps following an English attack in 1464. Repairs on the south side of the crossing area in the time of abbots Hall (1478–84) and Cranston (1484–88) were probably also at least partly necessitated by the damage then caused. There is a feeling that the community was determined not only to raise its church from the ashes, but to seize the chance to build something even more worthy.

This could not continue, however, and, after major destruction in 1523, 1544 and 1545, we see repairs of a kind that suggest it was simply becoming impossible to cope. It was perhaps after one of those that the roofs of the nave were lowered, and the consequences for the gallery stage must have been especially unfortunate because of the way the roofs were set below the arch-heads. Later still, the community was reduced to forming a chapel within the area of the crossing and transepts, and presumably much of the rest of the building would by then have been roofless. There must have been an almost equally disastrous situation at Holyrood, because in 1570 permission was given to demolish the eastern parts of the church which were still in ruins as a result of the English attacks. Evidently, after earlier valiant efforts, the English attacks of the 1540s left some houses unable to respond before the oncoming tide of the Reformation brought their religious life to an end.

CHAPTER EIGHT

The Monastic Buildings

The historical development of the claustral plan

In looking at the earliest monasteries it was noted that there was little apparent pre-ordained planning in their layout. A scattering of huts within the limits defined by a vallum could answer as places of prayer as well as of work and of habitation. However, the more tightly regulated and essentially communal way of monastic life represented by the rule of St Benedict encouraged a more systematic attitude to the layout of its buildings. As early as the mid-seventh century in parts of Europe there were the beginnings of an approach to planning in which the main buildings required by the monks were grouped around a central square space in a way that foreshadowed the cloister of the developed monastic plan. With the spread of the Benedictine rule fostered by the reforms of St Benedict of Aniane in the early ninth century, this tendency was given even greater momentum. Indeed, a famous plan which was probably drawn up in about 820 as a model for the abbot of St Gall in Switzerland already has many of the elements that were to become at least partly standardized for the houses of monks and canons in western Europe for the rest of the Middle Ages. Before looking at the buildings that made up a monastery in greater detail it may be helpful to consider the basic elements in such a layout.

The general arrangement of the buildings in a monastery

Much depended on the availability and position of a water supply to a monastery, because it was quickly appreciated that an enclosed community had to have a dependable source of water for drinking, preparing food, ensuring certain basic standards of hygiene and for carrying away waste. Where the water supply or the configuration of the site did not dictate otherwise, however, the church – usually the largest and most important structure of the complex – was on the north side of the main group of buildings (**colour plate 8**). In this position it did not block the daylight from the others, which were generally grouped around the other three sides of the square which formed the cloister, against the south flank of its nave. Although the cloister itself was an open space, it was surrounded by corridors, known as walks, which both interconnected all of the buildings and provided space for some of the more sedentary monastic activities (**73**).

These general principles underlay the planning of the majority of religious houses, but there were variants. This was especially the case in those smaller houses of Augustinian canons attached to existing churches, as at Pittenweem, where the cloister was apparently separated from the church. Another form

73 A reconstruction sketch of the main core of buildings at Arbroath Abbey (Duncan Peet).

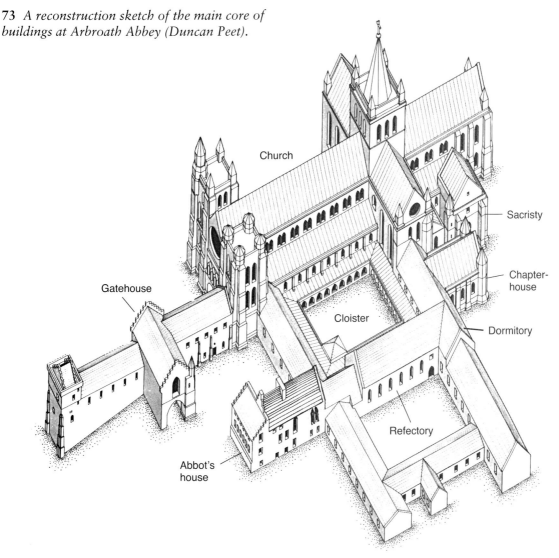

of variant is seen at Inchcolm, which is in fact the most complete surviving claustral complex in Scotland; but there the planning of the monastic buildings is atypical both because they are placed against an earlier church, and because the whole of the ground floor of the three ranges is given over to the walks (see **64** and **colour plate 13**). Eccentricities are also found in other orders, and at the Benedictine priory of Coldingham, for example, the cloister appears to have been against the flank of the choir rather than of the nave. But the most individual approach among any of the older orders was in houses

for the Carthusians, where each monk was given a small house-like cell within a garden of his own, and the church tended to be relatively small; it must be assumed that the Charterhouse at Perth would have been of this form.

Yet, allowing for such deviations, the weight of tradition behind the basic monastic layout was so strong that even the friars seem to have followed it so far as their frequently restricted urban sites would allow. It must be said that our knowledge of mendicant planning in Scotland is very limited, but the excavations at the Observant Franciscan house at Jedburgh and the Carmelite house at Linlithgow have revealed largely traditional plans on those sites at least.

In all but the most modest communities the buildings around the cloister formed only a main nucleus of the complex, and were essentially for the daily use of the monks or canons themselves. Around this core, but within the limits of a walled precinct, were large numbers of other buildings, depending on the scale, wealth, situation and order of the house. The interrelationships of these buildings were less predictable than were those of the buildings around the cloister; though some of them might be arranged around other enclosures, as at Arbroath, where there was a second cloister-like space immediately south of the cloister itself. Many of the outer buildings would have been accessible to a wider range of individuals, including the servants and lay officials who tended to proliferate, and who probably eventually outnumbered the monks. There would have been an infirmary for the old and sick monks, a residence for the head of the community where this was not part of the main complex, guest houses for the various ranks of visitors who might seek hospitality, administrative offices, and all the agricultural and industrial buildings required at the 'head office' of a wealthy estate.

Unfortunately our knowledge of these other buildings at the majority of Scottish monasteries is very limited. Very few have survived above ground, and where excavations have been carried out they have not generally extended very far beyond the main nucleus. It must also be said that most sites were excavated before archaeological techniques were as informative as they are today, and at a time when the main aim of the operation was simply to expose structural remains. The most complete excavation of recent years has been at Jedburgh Abbey, but this had to be limited to the area already in the care of the state, and it was on a site which had already been inadequately excavated earlier this century (**colour plate 14**). In view of such limitations, it was surprising how much evidence for the life of the canons could still be found, and it is a reminder of how much probably remains to be found elsewhere. Of other excavations, a number of the most invaluable have been at mendicant sites, including those at the Jedburgh Observant friary and several Carmelite friaries.

The east claustral range: the overall planning

The ground-floor rooms of the two-storeyed range on the east side of the cloister were almost invariably vaulted in order to provide a firm base for the dormitory on the floor above. The number of rooms at the lower level could vary, and we can seldom be entirely sure of all their uses. The main ones which might be found can be briefly listed. The sacristy was often part of the south range, but was really an adjunct of the church. It was the room where the vestments, vessels and books used at the services would be stored, and where the priests officiating at the altars could put on their vestments.

The chapter-house was the main meeting room of the community, and the second most important structure after the church itself. It took its name from a daily reading of a chapter of the monastic rule, but it was also a business room, and was the place where the monks confessed their sins; it was often a place where the head of the community chose to be buried. The slype was a passage which led through the range from the cloister to the area on its east. It could additionally be used as a *locutorium* or parlour where conversation was allowed. However, a separate parlour might also be provided, especially in Cistercian houses and the other orders influenced by them, as was perhaps the case at Glenluce and Sweetheart. Towards the outer end of the range there could be a

74 *The plan of Dryburgh Abbey.*

number of day rooms, including a room for the novices, and a warming room. The latter was the one room originally provided with a fireplace at which the monks or canons might warm themselves (an arrangement which perhaps more than any other highlights the difficulty of following in Scotland a rule written for monks in southern Italy). It probably tended to become a general common room.

At Dryburgh, where the late twelfth-century east range is particularly well-preserved, the sequence from the church at the north end to the outer end at the south seems to have been as follows: a sacristy next to the south transept, followed by a slype which also served as the inner parlour, and then by the chapter-house (**74** and **75** and **colour plate 9**). Beyond the chapter-house was the warming house and a second passage or slype, with another room beyond which may have been for the novices. It is likely that the undercroft of the latrine was at the end of the range since the drain runs here, but the outer extremity of the range has been lost. A slightly more compressed arrangement of rooms was to be seen in many houses. In the thirteenth-century range at Pluscarden, for example, the sequence was sacristy, chapter-house, slype or parlour, and day room, and

75 *The east monastic range at Dryburgh Abbey. The chapter-house is to the right, and the enlarged windows at the centre lit the warming room. The upper tier of windows was for the dormitory.*

there seems to have been a similar sequence at Dundrennan. In smaller houses, of course, there might be an even shorter sequence.

We must now give fuller consideration to some of the more important rooms within the east range.

The sacristy

Because of its relationship with the church, the sacristy was commonly immediately next to it. Indeed, at Cambuskenneth it appears to have been structurally a part of the transept rather than of the east range, and where no sacristy was provided within the east range a screened-off area within some other part of the church probably served the purpose. When the sacristy was in the east range it was usually entered directly from the church, but in some monasteries there were doorways from both the church and the cloister, as at Dryburgh, Pluscarden and Sweetheart. In such cases there may have been an internal subdivision of timber, with the eastern half being used as a sacristy and the western half as a library. Such a division was particularly common in Cistercian houses in the rest of Europe. Elsewhere the need for book storage within the cloister might be met by wall cupboards, as was the case at Arbroath and St Andrews.

In the later Middle Ages there was a vogue in Scotland for sacristies to be built against a flank of the choir but away from the cloister area. Examples are still to be seen at Arbroath and Pluscarden, and in both cases there was a treasury on an upper floor, in which the most valuable items could be safely stored. At Arbroath, where the sacristy-treasury is against the south choir chapel, its construction has been linked on the basis of heraldry with Abbot Paniter (*c.*1411–49), though it must be admitted that the architectural details look rather later than that (**76**). At Pluscarden, where it is on the north side of the choir, it can be ascribed to Prior Dunbar (1553–60). Nevertheless, sacristies continued to be provided within the east range, as at Crossraguel, where it is between the church and the chapter-house, and forms part of the rebuilding associated with Abbot Colin (1460–91). However, in that case a lack of correspondence between the wall shafts and the vault may suggest this space had been planned as a slype.

76 *The two-storeyed sacristy and treasury at Arbroath Abbey.*

The chapter-house

The most basic form for a chapter-house was a rectangular vaulted chamber within the body of the east range, as at Sweetheart. It usually had stone benches around the side walls on which the members of the community sat, and more prominent seats against the east wall for the head of the house and principal officers. In many cases it was given greater length by extending it eastwards beyond the range, as at Inchmahome and Lindores, and in some cases advantage was taken of this to place windows in part of the side walls. But a basic problem of a chamber within the range was that its position made it difficult to give sufficient architectural prominence to this most important of the claustral buildings. One way round this was to give it greater height by sinking the ground level, though this could only be done where the site sloped downwards, as at Dryburgh (**77**). In some other cases it seems it must have risen into the space devoted to the dormitory, as perhaps at Arbroath, though this must have created problems at the upper level of the range. An alternative was to accept the height limitation as a positive factor and to insert two rows of small piers to carry the vaulting. This was an approach particularly favoured by the Cistercians, and was adopted in the thirteenth-century chapter-house at the Cistercian house of Dundrennan, and possibly also at other houses of the order at Melrose and Newbattle (**78**).

At Newbattle, however, another device was also adopted to give greater scale: the chapter-house itself was pushed out beyond the east face of the range, presumably allowing it to rise to a greater height, with the

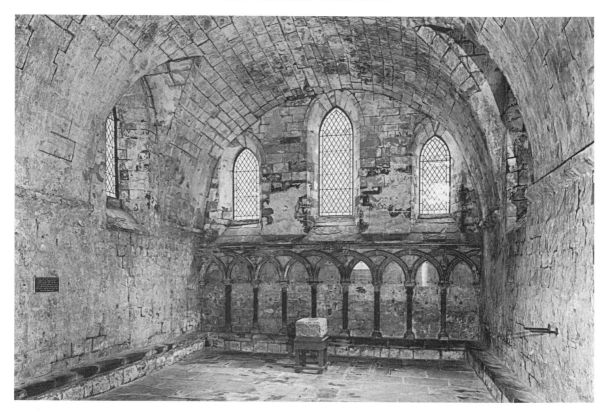

space inside the range itself being treated simply as a vestibule. This was also done at Balmerino, Holyrood, Inchcolm, Iona and St Andrews. The contrast between the lower space of the vestibule and the higher space of the chapter-house itself must have been highly attractive, as can still be seen in English examples of this approach such as Chester. At St Andrews, where the chapter-house and vestibule were originally part of the work completed by Prior White (1236–58), the former was rebuilt in time for Prior John of Forfar to be buried within it in 1321, and it was provided with arched seating recesses along the flanks. At Holyrood and Inchcolm – both of which were of the thirteenth century – the chapter-house was given a centralized octagonal plan, following an English fashion (79). Holyrood is only known from excavations, but its vault was carried on a central pier; the example at Inchcolm is still complete, and its smaller scale did not require a central pier. The only other known Scottish case of such an octagonal chapter-house is at the secular cathedral of Elgin.

In one sense such centralized structures may be seen as a more ambitious variant on another favoured type in Scotland, in which the chapter-house is a simple square within the body of the range, but has a central pier carrying four compartments of vaulting. Examples of this plan, dating from both the thirteenth and fifteenth centuries, are known of at Cambuskenneth, Crossraguel, Glenluce,

79 The octagonal chapter-house at Inchcolm Abbey, looking back towards the entrance doorway.

77 (Left, above) The chapter-house at Dryburgh Abbey. The decorative arcading of the east wall, where the abbot sat, was originally continued along the side walls as a painted design.

78 (Left, below) The interior of the chapter-house at Dundrennan Abbey. The central doorway is flanked by two open windows, and the vaulting was carried on two rows of piers.

Jedburgh and Pluscarden, and that at Balmerino must have been similar except that it was outside the range. The examples at Crossraguel, Glenluce and Pluscarden still survive complete and are very handsome spaces. Those at Crossraguel and Glenluce (80) are particularly closely related to each other, and the similarity of the window tracery suggests that the late fifteenth- or early sixteenth-century master mason at Glenluce was directly copying the design of Abbot Colin's mason at Crossraguel. In at least one case, that of Jedburgh, we know from excavation that this plan was adopted only after two earlier phases in which the chapter-house had projected eastwards from the range.

80 *The square chapter-house at Glenluce Abbey. The vaulting is carried on a central pier.*

In earlier chapter-houses the favoured treatment of the entrance from the cloister walk was a central doorway flanked by a window on each side, as is seen in late twelfth-century form at Dryburgh (81). Thirteenth-century variants on this same idea are visible at Culross, Dundrennan and Pluscarden, while at Kilwinning it seems that the same idea was taken up again at the very end of the Middle Ages in a design that was closely based on twelfth-century prototypes. By that stage, however, most chapter-houses had an entrance doorway without flanking windows; at Crossraguel it was not even centrally placed.

The dormitory

The whole of the upper floor of the east range, from the flank of the south transept in a major church to the reredorter or latrine at the outer end, was usually given over to the dormitory. The only house where a dormitory survives complete is at Inchcolm which, as part of the thoroughgoing approach to fire-proofing there, is covered by a pointed barrel vault, although this is likely to have been unusual (82). Clues to the arrangement of a more typical dormitory are to be seen at Dryburgh, though there allowance has to be made for its less complete state, as well as for alterations that were later made to it to adapt it for residential use. In some cases the dormitory occupied only part of the upper floor, as seems to have been the case in the rebuilt ranges at both Crossraguel and Inchmahome, though in both those examples this may not reflect the original disposition.

The positions of the day and night stairs to and from the dormitory could vary. In many cases the access from the dormitory into the church was a spiral stair in a corner of the transept, as at Kilwinning and Arbroath, though this can never have been easy to negotiate at night-time, and at St Andrews we find that a spiral stair was later replaced by a more stately flight within the transept. Straight flights, or the positions of them, are also to be seen at Dryburgh, Glenluce, Iona,

81 *The entrance to the chapter-house at Dryburgh Abbey, with the central doorway flanked by a pair of two-light windows.*

Pluscarden and Sweetheart, among other examples. At Inchmahome, where the dormitory did not extend up to meet the church, a straight stair and covered corridor were evidently contrived beyond the chapter-house, and there is something similar at Inchcolm, where the dormitory abutted the site of the old church.

The position of the day stair is less frequently known. At Lindores, Dryburgh (83) and St Andrews it simply came down within the body of the range, at ninety degrees to its main axis, to a door opening into the east cloister walk. It was usually quite spacious, though at Balmerino it was within the thickness of the north wall of the chapter-house vestibule and was thus very narrow. At Sweetheart, however, it seems it came down into the south range, thus leaving the floor space within the dormitory unencumbered. At Inchmahome there was an even more unusual arrangement: since the east cloister walk was within the body of the range, by placing the stair against the west wall of the dormitory it was possible for it to be brought down at the junction of the east and south walks (see **50** and **64**).

The reredorter

The reredorter, or latrine, was always designed to be reached from the dormitory, and could be a building of surprisingly magnificent scale for one that was destined for such a mundane purpose. The relationship with the dormitory depended mainly on the line of the drain. At Dunfermline the reredorter was on the east side of the dormitory range, running parallel with it, while at St

82 *The dormitory at Inchcolm Abbey, looking northwards. The windows on the left look down into the cloister.*

83 *The warming room at Dryburgh Abbey. At the far end can be seen the remains of the stair between the dormitory and the cloister that was used during the day-time.*

structure in the hierarchy of buildings. It was often at first-floor level, as at Crossraguel and Iona. This was perhaps partly because of the analogy with the upper room in which the Last Supper was taken, though parallels with halls in secular residences – which tended to be raised above a basement – must not be forgotten. Practical considerations also played a part, and at several houses the slope of the site meant it had to be elevated on a vaulted undercroft for it even to be at the level of the cloister, as at Culross, Deer and Dryburgh. At Dunfermline the slope of the site was so great that there were two levels of undercroft there (**84**).

Most frequently the refectory ran parallel to the church, and thus occupied most of the range, unless the cloister was unusually large like that at St Andrews. In some Cistercian houses, however, including Dundrennan, Glenluce, Melrose and Sweetheart, it came to be set at ninety degrees to the cloister. One consideration behind this change of axis may have been that it could be larger. But it may also have been important that other buildings, the warming room on one side and the kitchen on the other, could be visited in the course of the weekly procession around the monastic buildings without leaving the cloister. In non-Cistercian houses, however, the kitchen was often placed at a little distance from the other buildings around the cloister, both because of the risk of fire and to avoid the smells which resulted from cooking over open fires.

The most complete refectory is at Inchcolm but, as with the dormitory, it is not typical in its pointed barrel-vaulted covering. Important remains of refectories are also found at Ardchattan, Crossraguel, Dryburgh, and in partly restored state at Iona and St Andrews. But undoubtedly the most impressive survivor is that at Dunfermline, towards which Robert I was making donations shortly before his death in 1329 (see **37** and **38** and **colour plates 10** and **11**). The south and

Andrews, Inchcolm and Iona it projected at right angles from the end of it, and at Dundrennan and Melrose it projected at right angles from the east face of the range. Usually the individual cubicles must have been directly over the drain, but at Inchcolm it was designed to be washed out by the sea, with the consequence that it had to be extended when the beach level rose. Later reredorters, as at Crossraguel and Inchmahome, may have been rather smaller in scale, and in some cases it is possible they emptied into cesspits rather than into the main drain.

The refectory range

The main room in the range facing the church across the cloister, was the refectory or frater, which was the third most important

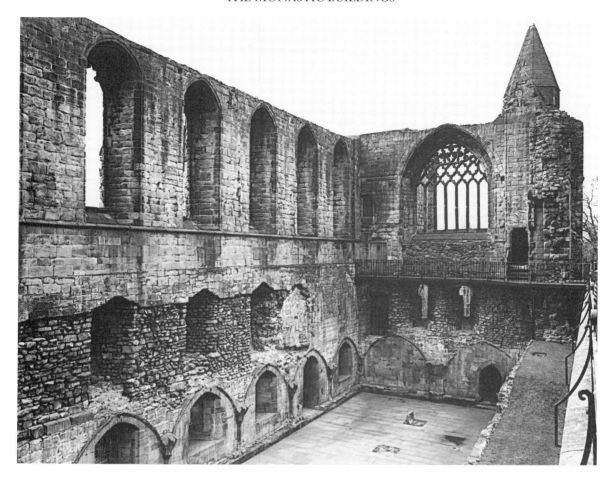

west walls of this magnificent structure survive virtually complete, and the tracery of their large windows is a fascinating indicator that English influences were still paramount in Scotland in the earlier fourteenth century, even after the first bruising phase of the Wars of Independence. Built into the south wall is a handsome pulpit, from which appropriate readings were made to the assembled monks during meals. It was projected outwards on an arch between the buttresses, and covered by delicate vaulting. Other refectory pulpits survive at Inchcolm and Ardchattan, in the latter case embodied within the post-Reformation house which occupies much of the site of the monastic buildings.

Near the entrance to the refectory, most frequently within the south or west cloister walk, was the lavatory, or washing place,

84 *The refectory at Dunfermline Abbey, looking westwards (compare with 37). Because of the slope of the land the refectory itself had to be raised above two levels of vaulted undercrofts, both of which have now collapsed. The main floor level was at the line of the ledge below the top tier of windows.*

where the monks ritually washed their hands before taking food. Usually this was a simple trough within a recess, as at Inchcolm. But in other cases there may have been some form of fountain. At Melrose the base of a circular fountain is still to be seen within the foundations of a pavilion projecting into the cloister, and there was also a pavilion in the southwest angle of the cloister at Arbroath.

The warming room and kitchen

For most orders the preferred place for the warming room, or calefactory, was towards the outer end of the east range. The positions of fireplaces at Dryburgh, Inchmahome and St Andrews still show the location of this room in the east range at those houses. The oddest site for a room serving this function is at Inchcolm, where the thirteenth-century octagonal chapter-house was heightened in the fifteenth century to provide a room leading off the dormitory and in this room a fireplace is the most prominent feature. But whether this can strictly be described as a warming room is debatable. In some of those Cistercian houses which had the refectory at

right angles to the south range, as has been said, the warming room may have been to the east of the refectory, and at Dundrennan the base of what seems to have been a fireplace has been found in this position.

Few monastic kitchens have survived in more than fragmentary state. One of the best is that at Dunfermline, which is across the far side of the roadway into the precinct from the refectory, in which position it also served the adjacent guest house. It was raised above a vaulted undercroft, though the steeply sloping terrain meant that it was still two storeys lower than the refectory, which was eventually reached by way of a tortuous route through the later gatehouse. There seem to have been at least four fireplaces,

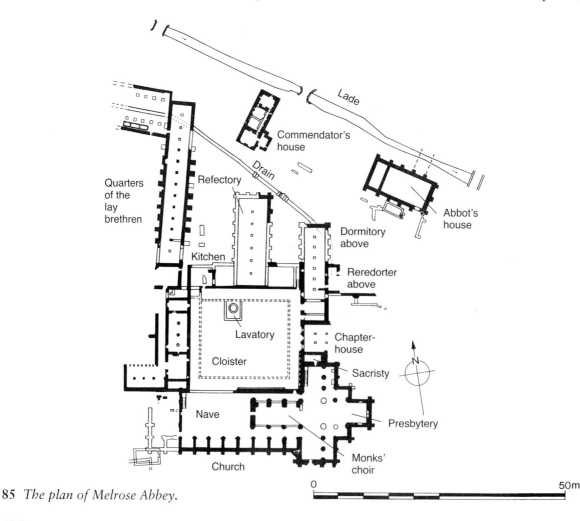

85 *The plan of Melrose Abbey.*

two of which were built out on arches between the buttresses. Significant traces of the kitchens also survive at Arbroath and Melrose, where they are to the west of the refectory. At Arbroath the fireplaces were apparently set diagonally across the western corners of the room; a second kitchen was later fitted up in the undercroft of the abbot's house.

The west claustral range

The uses of the range on the west of the cloister were the least predictable; sometimes, indeed, a west range was simply dispensed with altogether, as may originally have been the case at Dryburgh and Oronsay. One usual feature in this range was a slype or outer parlour, giving access from the cloister to the main courtyard of the abbey, where conversation might be allowed between monks and visitors under certain circumstances. Well-preserved examples of outer parlours are to be seen at Culross and Kelso. The position of the outer parlour reflects the fact that the west range was best placed to serve those functions which required contact with the greater world, since it was usually the side which was nearest to the main gateway into the precinct. Thus the cellarer, who was in charge of a monastery's provisions, often had his stores here, so that they could be brought in without disturbance to the rest of the community. In a number of houses the head of the community had his residence in this range, so that he was both close to his monks, as the rule required, but also at the point of closest contact with the world beyond the precinct. In some cases there may even have been a guest house here.

As in so many other respects, the Cistercians developed a use of their own for the west side of the cloister. It was here that the lay brethren were usually placed, with their refectory and other day rooms at ground-floor level and their dormitory above. The truncated stumps of these rooms are still to be seen at Culross. The lay brethren might also have their workshops in this area and, to insulate the cloister from the noise they created, a narrow open space known as the lane was sometimes placed between the cloister and the west range. This was originally the case at Melrose though, after recruitment of lay brethren had ended in the fourteenth century, the lane was absorbed into the area of the cloister (85). Melrose has the remains of a particularly extensive series of buildings for the lay brethren, which extend over 100m (330ft) northwards from the church, but care was taken to separate it from the main processional entrance in the west front of the church by a blank screen wall.

The cloister walks

The covered walks around the edges of the cloister most frequently simply ran alongside the church and three ranges of monastic buildings, and were covered by lean-to single-pitch roofs. But there were exceptions. At Inchcolm the south, east and west walks occupied the whole of the ground floor of the three ranges, while a north walk was created within the lower parts of the nave and tower of the original church, which by that stage had been replaced by a new church further east. At a later stage the old church was put to yet other uses, and a lean-to range built against it, though little of this now remains. At some other Augustinian houses the walks were also at least partly within the body of the ranges, as on the east and west sides of the cloister at Inchmahome, and the same later happened on the south side of the cloister at Jedburgh. In England such an arrangement was more common in the houses of the mendicants, but the only Scottish friary where this may have happened is at Jedburgh, where there is a possibility that one walk was within the range.

86 The restored cloister arcades at Iona Abbey, which are carried on slender pairs of shafts.

The walls which carried the lean-to roofs were generally of fairly slight construction, being pierced by a large number of open arches, and they have not survived well. In the twelfth and early thirteenth centuries the arches were often carried on pairs of slender shafts, as is still to be seen in restored form in the cloister of Iona, though the convex form of the shafts there cannot have been typical (86). Elsewhere some of the caps or bases for such paired shafts have survived, as at Cambuskenneth, Dunfermline, Melrose and Scone, showing that they also were of this type. Later cloister arcades might be as plain or as complex as the house could afford. At Inchcolm and Oronsay there were simple regularly-spaced round-arched openings, though at the latter some of the arcades were reconstructed with triangular heads formed by laying one slab against another. Sometimes stone seats were provided within the window embrasures, as at both Inchcolm and Inchmahome, the latter having its openings subdivided by mullions.

A lighter treatment of the arcade walls must have existed at many houses. At Glenluce, for example, where part of the arcade outside the chapter-house entrance has been reconstructed from surviving fragments, there was a sequence of narrow arched openings. Perhaps the grandest cloister for which we have evidence would have been that at Melrose, though it is doubtful if it was ever completed as planned in the fourteenth and fifteenth centuries (87). The chief pointers to what was intended are the decorative blind arcading against the west wall of the south transept and the north wall of the nave. As first started the walls were divided into bays by arched recesses with elaborately-crocketed ogee hood-mouldings. These arches presumably would have had corresponding arches opening on to the cloister. After the first bay in the nave, however, they were replaced by less expensive shallow trifoliate arches, the only exception to which was a more complex arch marking the seat occupied by the abbot at the daily reading before Compline from Cassian's Collations.

The lodgings of abbots, priors and commendators

St Benedict had said that the head of a monastery should live in common with his brethren. But this became impracticable as the leaders of the greater monasteries were expected to play an increasingly active part in the running of the state, both as representatives of land-holding bodies and as leading members of the nation's literate élite. Much

87 The decorative arcading at the base of the north transept wall at Melrose Abbey was originally at the back of the cloister walks. The roofs were supported by the corbels and slots to be seen in the walls.

of the architectural history of the residences provided for monastic heads is one of trying to balance the requirement for a separate residence of fitting scale, while still paying lip service to the idea of that residence being part of the main monastic complex.

The finest and most complete abbot's residence to survive is that at Arbroath, the nucleus of which is a first-floor hall dating from the years around 1200, which originally projected westwards from the junction of the west and south ranges around the cloister (88). In this position it was linked with the monks' refectory, and probably originally shared their kitchen, but was also close to

88 *The abbot's house at Arbroath Abbey. Originally it extended no further west than the chimney stack at the centre of this view. In its final state the main entrance was at first-floor level, to the left of the triplet of three large rectangular windows.*

the main gateway which opened into the precinct. By about 1500 there had developed around this hall a far more imposing residence, with an entrance gallery approached by an external flight of steps, which gave access to the hall, a new bed chamber beyond, and a stair to the upper floor and basement. There were also a closet and a gallery off the bed chamber and a supply of latrines.

In several monasteries the abbot's house was linked to the other buildings by the reredorter block at the end of the dormitory, which was yet another way of preserving the letter – if not the spirit – of communal life. This was the case at Crossraguel, Deer, Inchcolm, Iona and Jedburgh, and may have been so elsewhere, including Holyrood, Kinloss, Oronsay and Pluscarden. In most cases the residence extended eastwards from the latrine block, but in others it ran parallel to the refectory, as at Iona, Jedburgh and probably at Holyrood. Another position

for the abbot's house can be seen at Dunfermline, where it was probably to the north of the abbey, abutting the precinct wall. Alternatively, as at Balmerino and Melrose where the cloister was itself on the north side of the church, it seems the abbot's house was to the north-east of the main complex. At Melrose, where only the foundations remain, the house was probably of thirteenth-century construction and consisted of a buttressed ground-floor hall of four bays with a chamber at each end. Only a vault of the undercroft survives at Balmerino, which is probably considerably later in date.

The house at Balmerino may have been one manifestation of a renewed late medieval enthusiasm for building grand residences for abbots, or for the commendators who were replacing so many of them. Abbot Andrew Hunter of Melrose (c.1444–71) is thought to have built a new house there, to replace its thirteenth-century predecessor, and it eventually formed the basis of the later commendator's house. He was a keen builder and certainly constructed a handsome tower as the core of another residence for himself on Melrose's grange at Mauchline in Ayrshire. A tower was also built to contain the main chambers of the residence at Crossraguel, apparently by Abbot Colin (1460–91), attached to which was the first-floor hall range of the earlier residence, with a kitchen block at ninety degrees to it (89). Among other abbatial or commendatorial residences

89 *The plan of Crossraguel Abbey.*

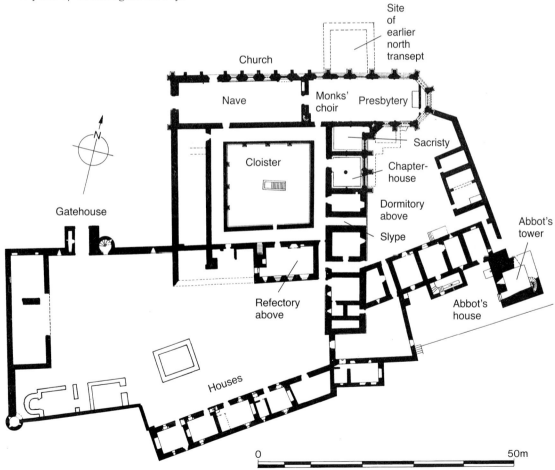

built at this period, at both Beauly and Kinloss Robert Reid is known to have raised handsome houses for himself in the early sixteenth century, and parts of the latter still survive.

In the last decades of Scottish monasticism there is some confusion about a number of the residences which may have been built for commendators. At several abbeys the claustral ranges were themselves adapted as residences, as may be seen in the east ranges at Balmerino and Dryburgh and the west range at Inchaffray, for example. It is usually assumed that such radical changes could only have been carried out after the Reformation, when conventual life was defunct; but there is the possibility that some such changes were made even before then, since it seems that many monasteries were no longer using their buildings as originally intended. However, more research is needed before we can be certain about this.

Guest houses

Guest houses were built by monasteries as part of the duty of providing hospitality for travellers. The most important short-term visitors would probably have been housed by the abbot within his own residence, with others expecting to be accommodated in a way that was appropriate to their social status. One of the chief burdens of hospitality was towards the family of the founder and their successors, who would continue to feel a proprietorial interest in the house. This could become a distinctly onerous burden when the founder or his successor was the monarch, and especially so where the monastery was in a situation that was likely to be frequently visited. In a number of such cases it seems that the king might have had buildings constructed to meet his needs, and these might progressively develop into major royal residences.

This certainly happened at Holyrood,

where the royal guest house not only grew into a large quadrangular complex, but also eventually took over some of the buildings that had been created for the canons; at Holyrood the resultant palace was to survive the abbey, and still remains in use (**90**). There was a similar development at Dunfermline, where the magnificent guest house above the Tower Burn, adjoining the gate into the inner precinct, is at least partly contemporary with the nearby refectory (**91**). The way it was later expanded in the late sixteenth century to form part of a palace for Anne of Denmark – which also encompassed some of the monastic buildings – could indicate that guest house had been intended for royal use from the start.

The little we know of other guest houses suggests they were generally of more modest

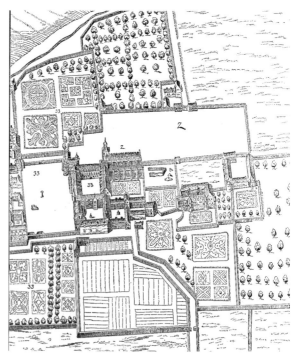

90 *An aerial view of the abbey and palace of Holyrood by the mid-seventeenth century. The nave of the abbey church is towards the back, with the palace that grew up on the west side of the cloister towards left of centre in this view (Gordon of Rothiemay).*

91 *The monastic guest house at Dunfermline Abbey, as later converted into a palace for Queen Anne of Denmark.*

scale. This fact, together with their planning, has also made them candidates for later adaptation. At Inverkeithing, for example, the guest house of the Franciscan friary, probably dating from not long after 1384, now serves as a local museum. Similarly, at Arbroath a heavily-restored two-storeyed hall and chamber block against the precinct wall, which may have been one of the abbey's hospices, was used by the burgh for many years. There is a similar plan underlying a superficially eighteenth-century house to the west of Melrose Abbey and, since this house has unexpectedly thick walls, it is one possibility that it represents a medieval guest house that has been adapted for later domestic use. In other cases there may have been guest houses within the main claustral complex itself, and this is one possible use for the upper floor of the west range at Inchcolm, and perhaps even for the upper level of the first church after it had been abandoned for worship. The mid-thirteenth century foundations at the south-west corner of Jedburgh's cloister could also have served this purpose.

Other buildings within the precinct

It has to be said that our understanding of the layout and range of building types within the precinct at most Scottish monastic houses is inadequate, and there is still great scope for archaeological and documentary research in this area. Current knowledge of even so important a building as the infirmary is severely limited.

The earliest example of an infirmary so far traced may be that of the late twelfth century at Kelso, where excavations in the 1970s located to the south-east of the cloister a large hall on a north–south axis, with an aisle on its east side carried on alternating cylindrical and octagonal piers. At Melrose part of the infirmary hall of the lay brethren, which could be of the thirteenth century, probably remains at the north-west corner of their quarters; this must have been a splendid structure, with aisles down both sides. Buildings have also been identified as infirmaries at a number of other houses, albeit often on little more evidence than their position to the east of the cloister. That at Iona is a simple rectangular structure, which has been entirely rebuilt as part of the modern restoration. At Deer it has been suggested that a U-shaped grouping of ranges was the infirmary. It may be that a complex of related plan to the south-east of the cloister at Glenluce served the same function, and that the structures usually identified as the infirmary were instead part of the abbot's lodging.

A number of other buildings which might stand within the precinct must be briefly listed here. At Arbroath we have part of the hall that was used as the regality court house, in which decisions were taken concerning all the estates and the people attached to them over which the abbot exercised authority. Elsewhere, however, as at Melrose, it seems the regality court house was outside the precinct. At Crossraguel the main enclosure to the south of the abbey church has an unusual row of small houses along one side, which it has been suggested were occupied by corrodiars, that is individuals who had paid for or otherwise acquired the right to live at the expense of the community. But it is perhaps just as likely that they were occupied by some monks of the community, at a period when it seems that increasing numbers of monks and canons were allowed their own houses and gardens, along with a portion of the monastic income.

Very few of the agricultural buildings that might be expected within the precinct have survived, though there is part of what could have been a barn to the north of the cloister at Balmerino, and the site of a barn is known at St Andrews. The sites of corn mills are also known with reasonable certainty at St Andrews and Melrose. In the former case there was a dam for the necessary head of water nearby, and there were also bakehouses, while the latter was next to the canal which brought the water supply into the precinct.

Water supply and drainage

It has already been said that a supply of fresh water was of paramount importance at a monastic site, and could even lead to the domestic buildings being placed on the north rather than the south side of the church. This happened at Melrose, where the water engineering is relatively well understood (92). The river Tweed was about 400m (1310ft) north of the site chosen for the abbey church, and to obtain a supply of water a canal or

92 *The main drain at Melrose Abbey. It was originally completely covered over, but only a few of the lintel stones now survive.*

lade was excavated from a point well upstream from the abbey, returning to the river in due course. From that lade was taken another loop, which formed the main drain, and which flowed through the monastic buildings, interconnecting the latrines of the lay brethren and monks, and into which were fed many subsidiary drains. Part of the lade, together with extensive stretches of the network of drains have been excavated and are still to be seen; they provide the clearest evidence for the enormous care that was taken in the planning of these arrangements.

At Melrose the walls of much of the drain are relatively roughly constructed, but where it runs through the reredorter it is built of good ashlar masonry, so that there was no risk of the waste collecting. Melrose was not alone in this, and at several other houses, including Dunfermline and St Andrews, the same care can be seen in the construction of the section of drain that ran through the latrines. The finest drain of any so far discovered, however, is that at Paisley, parts of which are quite exquisitely constructed with polished ashlar to the floor and walls, and finely built arches to carry the roofing.

To obtain a supply of fresh water for drinking and cooking many houses resorted to laying runs of piping. Extents of lead piping have been found at several sites, including Arbroath, Melrose and the infirmary hall at Kelso. Excavations at Lesmahagow in 1978 located a section of lead piping which must have fed the lavatory in the west cloister range before passing on to other parts; it was also found to be linked with a carefully-planned network of clay-lined drains. At other monasteries the water supply was carried through interlocking earthenware pipes, as was the case at Glenluce, and there the eminently practical approach to its planning is seen in the inspection chambers provided at the junctions (**93**).

Gatehouses and precinct walls

Monastic precincts were usually defined by clear boundaries, and for a number of the earlier monasteries existing fortifications such as those of Iron Age fortresses may have been pressed into service for at least part of the vallum. Even with some of the later houses earlier works may have been partly reused, and at Coupar Angus, for example, it is not impossible that one boundary originated as part of a Roman camp. The principal function of these boundaries was probably to emphasize the enclosure and separateness of the community. Nevertheless, defence must have been an additional consideration, particularly after some of the abbeys had become so enormously wealthy – with all the frictions that inevitably created – and

some boundary walls acquired a distinctly militaristic air.

Imposing stretches of precinct wall are still to be seen at Arbroath, Crossraguel, Pluscarden, St Andrews (**colour plate 15**) and Sweetheart, while there are fine monastic gates at Coupar Angus, Crossraguel, Dunfermline, Pittenweem, St Andrews and Whithorn. Except in the more fully enclosed orders, such as the Cistercians, the main gate into the inner precinct was often positioned to the south-west of the church. In this way a relatively open outer court was left in front of the west facade and the north flank of the church, where were respectively the main processional entrance and the principal doorway for the layfolk. This is certainly the position of the main gate at Arbroath, Crossraguel, Dunfermline and St Andrews. But there would be other gates as well, and at St Andrews three other gates still survive, while there are remains of one other of the gates at Dunfermline. Chapels were sometimes associated with the gatehouses, presumably for the benefit of travellers, and there are references to such a chapel over one of the three or four gates of Melrose.

At Arbroath the precinct wall comes straight out from the south-west corner of

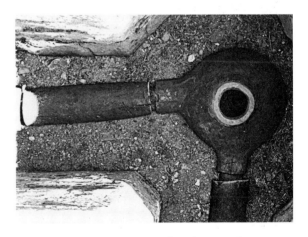

93 *One of the inspection chambers in the system of water pipes at Glenluce Abbey.*

the church, and is punctuated by the splendid two-storeyed gatehouse, before terminating at a great tower where it originally changed direction (94). As now seen the wall, gate and tower date chiefly from the fourteenth and fifteenth centuries. Although the wall-head defences, with machicolations to the gate and tower, may have been intended chiefly to create a fine impression, they would also have been eminently serviceable in an emergency. The same is true of the walls at St Andrews, where a considerable proportion of the original circuit survives, including thirteen regularly-spaced rectangular or semicircular towers (95). The earliest parts may be of the later fourteenth century, but they were heightened and strengthened by priors John and Patrick Hepburn in the later fifteenth and earlier

sixteenth centuries, at which time shot-holes were provided. In their final state they offer a magnificent statement of the wealth and standing of Scotland's most important religious house.

95 (Right) *The towered precinct wall at St Andrews Cathedral Priory. A change in the character of the masonry can be seen at about mid-height, showing where it was heightened in the late Middle Ages.*

94 (Below) *The surviving stretch of precinct wall at Arbroath Abbey, to the west of the abbey church. It has the main gatehouse at its mid-point, and a square tower at the change in angle.*

CHAPTER NINE

The Religious Houses and the Reformation

The state of the religious houses in the later Middle Ages

The Scottish Reformation was accomplished through the parliament of 1560, which abolished the mass as the principal form of worship, and rejected the authority of the papacy over the church. But the Reformation was in fact a more progressive process than that statement might suggest, with events unfolding over several decades to either side of 1560.

There can be no doubt that by the early sixteenth century there was much that was wrong with the church, and there were certainly critics of the monks, canons and friars. But, in making any judgement of religious life in the late Middle Ages it is important that a fair balance is struck, and that the criticisms of the reformers are not accepted unquestioningly. It must not be forgotten that there were houses where a high standard still prevailed. The Perth Charterhouse was certainly one, and the convent of Dominican nuns at Sciennes in Edinburgh was another. In addition, there were several houses with vigorous leaders who reintroduced a stricter discipline and brought fresh heart to their communities. Chief among these were Kinloss under Abbot Thomas Crystal, and later under Abbot Robert Reid (who was also eventually to have Beauly under his wing), and Cambuskenneth under Abbot

Alexander Myln. Some sections of the mendicant orders were also in a healthy state, since there had been a shake-up of the Dominican friars in the early sixteenth century, and it is likely that most of the Observant Franciscan houses were still in relatively fine fettle. Indeed, it may be that the friars were seen as one of the greatest threats to the reforming party, since one of the first blows of the Reformation, the 'Beggar's Summons' of 1559, was particularly directed against them.

There was also a growing realization in other quarters of the church that something had to be done to confront the problems, and this did at least result in a visitation of the houses of the Cistercian order in the early 1530s, in an attempt to eradicate the most obvious abuses. But, although some changes were introduced at Cistercian Deer and Coupar Angus it may be doubted how much was achieved across the board, since there was resistance to change by most of the abbeys visited. Rather confusingly, although James V had been anxious that these visitations should take place, he then defended the abbeys against some of the criticisms made on the grounds that allowances were not being made for Scottish conditions.

Yet, whatever allowances are made, it seems that the lives of most monks and canons, and perhaps also of many friars, were comfortable and spiritually undemanding. The food was generally plentiful, the accommodation spacious, an adequate financial competence was provided, and there was genial company; all of which suggests parallels with the life of an eighteenth-century fellow in a well-endowed English university college.

One of the most clearly identifiable problems which beset houses of both monks and canons was the way increasing numbers of them were headed not by abbots or priors, but by commendators – though this in itself was perhaps more a symptom than a cause of decline. These commendators were men appointed by the king in reward for their services to, or relationship with, the crown, and whose chief interest in the houses under their control was as a source of income. The first stage in this process was probably when non-monastic clergy began to be appointed, though initially these always took monastic vows and so became full abbots. But later many appointees were not even in clerical orders at the time of their appointment. Some, indeed, were under-age royal bastards, though they would not come into full possession of their commendatorship until they were of age.

All such commendators took orders after their appointment, if not before, though they had no intention of becoming monks, and in very few cases was their appointment to the benefit of the abbeys. Though many built handsome houses for themselves within the monastic precinct, few took a close interest in the running of the monastery. In truth, the situation probably had little immediate impact on the monks or canons, since the day-to-day running would be left to the prior in an abbey, or the sub-prior in a priory, as had already been the case when the abbots or priors had been absent; it was perhaps only when a commendator starved his abbey of resources that the monks were stung into action, as happened at Melrose in 1556, when the church was said to be becoming unusable. But the lack of positive leadership inevitably took its toll on morale and discipline, at a time when those were sadly needed.

Another significant factor in the decades leading up to the Reformation may have been a sense of complacency within the religious orders that was fostered by all the signs that James V had little thought of breaking with Rome, as did his uncle, Henry VIII of England. Since at least 1487, in the time of James III, successive popes had granted Scottish kings ever more authority within the national church, and they were likely to grant yet more autonomy as an encouragement to remain loyal once Henry declared himself head of the English church in 1531. The situation was more changeable after the death of James V in 1542, particularly under the regency of the Earl of Arran, and church leaders began to take a slightly more positive approach to the need for reforming well-attested abuses.

Nevertheless, even at this late stage, it was by no means inevitable that the storm would break. There was certainly an increase in the feuing of church property as a way of reaping short-term profits from it, and the fear of reform must have been a factor in this. Even so, at several houses there is evidence of construction operations well into the sixteenth century. Some of this building, at Jedburgh and Holyrood for example, was necessitated by devastating English attacks in the 1540s. But at others it was in response to a continuing wish to provide fitting buildings, though it must be admitted that many of those buildings were chiefly aimed at increasing domestic comfort, as with the abbot's house at Arbroath.

The Reformation

When the Reformation did come, the main effect on the majority of the monks and canons was that they were no longer able to perform their main function, the chanting of the canonical hours and the celebration of the mass – although many must have continued covertly to do so. But there was no question of the monasteries ceasing to exist as landed corporations, and those monks and canons who were content to spend the remainder of their days within the familiar walls of their conventual buildings were usually left to do so. In general, they also continued to enjoy their portion of the monastic income, although there may have been delays, as when in 1563 the monks of Melrose said they were three years in arrears. Despite such problems they even escaped the arrangements made in 1561 to withhold one third of all ecclesiastical stipends in order to fund the reformed church and to provide the crown with additional revenue.

Similarly, commendators continued to be appointed and to enjoy their rights in the monastic estates, though their office was now completely secular. Eventually many commendators were in the fortunate position of having those estates granted to them on a permanent basis. There must have been some alarm in 1587 when, on attaining his majority, James VI passed an Act of Annexation, by which he laid claim to all ecclesiastical estates on the basis that they had been alienated to the church by his royal predecessors, and this act is still the basis on which some monastic remains are regarded as crown property. Nevertheless, James recognized that the granting of those estates was one of the best means of buying support and, as the monastic communities died out, many were erected into temporal lordships. Indeed, those estates still form the nucleus of the land-holdings of some of Scotland's aristocratic families.

The impact of the Reformation on the buildings

Architecturally, the impact of the Reformation was varied. 'Cleansing' of the trappings of the older forms of worship was often more destructive than the reformers claimed was their intention, particularly when it extended to removal of window glass and lead with the consequent ingress of wind and water. In general it was perhaps the case that the more accessible a building was, the more likely it was to suffer damage in the first throes of reformist fervour. Things were therefore particularly black for the mendicants since, quite apart from any intellectual threat they may have posed to the programmes of the reformers, most of their sites were in the middle of populous burghs. At Perth, for example, following John Knox's sermon of 11 May 1559, the houses of the Dominicans and Franciscans were so ravaged by the mob that Knox himself admitted that little remained apart from the walls. Nevertheless, a number of mendicant churches did survive through being put to alternative uses, and in 1561 it was suggested that the undemolished friaries should be converted to educational uses. At Glasgow and Aberdeen the Dominican and Observant churches were soon to be used by the universities (though they have since been lost), while at Elgin and Queensferry the Observant and Carmelite churches were put to a variety of more or less appropriate uses.

The long-term outlook was also bad for those monastic churches that did not have an established parochial use, such as St Andrews, where the church of the cathedral priory was abandoned by the archbishop in favour of the nearby parish church (96). There the cathedral had been particularly thoroughly cleansed after Knox had preached against the old ways in the parish church, though a late sixteenth-century aerial view of the city suggests the fabric remained upstanding for some decades to come. At Arbroath the parish church for the local community was a short distance away at St Vigeans and, though the abbey seems to have been briefly used for reformed worship, it was soon abandoned. In both those cases ruination of the churches soon followed abandonment, and by the later seventeenth century the engravings of Slezer show they were already in almost as advanced a state of ruination as now.

Nevertheless, considerably more of the monastic churches and their associated conventual buildings remained in use after the Reformation than is generally appreciated – at least for a while. At Arbroath the abbot's house remained in use until earlier this century, and some fine post-medieval houses, such as Newbattle or Ardchattan, still have the conventual buildings of a monastic house at their core. Among the various places where there is evidence of the conventual buildings having been adapted as residences for the commendators or for later owners are Benedictine May, Cluniac Paisley, Tironensian Arbroath, Cistercian Balmerino, Culross

and Melrose, Pluscarden (originally Valliscaulian but later Benedictine), Augustinian Inchaffray, Inchcolm, Pittenweem and St Andrews, and Premonstratensian Dryburgh. In a number of those cases it is at least a possibility that some of the alterations had been started before the Reformation to adapt the buildings for changed forms of monastic life. On a grander scale, the royal palaces of Holyrood and Dunfermline grew out of the abbeys in which they had their origins.

Turning from the conventual buildings to the churches, several are still wholly or partly in use for worship, including Coldingham, Paisley, Culross, Monymusk, Pittenweem, Fearn and Torphichen (97), while such as the abbeys of Iona (98) and Pluscarden and the friaries of Elgin and South Queensferry have been restored in modern times. But the number of churches where either the choir or the nave was adapted for reformed parochial worship was originally considerably greater, while others were brought back into use several decades after the Reformation. This happened at Culross, where it was only in 1633

96 St Andrews Cathedral by the later seventeenth century, demonstrating how it had been almost reduced to its present state by little more than a century after the Reformation.

97 *The post-Reformation church on the site of the nave of Torphichen Preceptory. The medieval transepts and tower of the Preceptory church are on the left.*

that it was decided the abbey was more conveniently placed than the parish church (see **47**). An even more extraordinary case is Melrose, where the early seventeenth-century decision to use the old monastic choir as the parish church involved the insertion of masses of masonry in a way that leaves little doubt that it was not the beauties of the medieval abbey that were the attraction to the parishioners.

Assessing the architectural impact

Many of the churches which had been retained for worship or brought back into use were only abandoned as late as the eighteenth or nineteenth centuries. Sometimes the motives which led to such late abandonment were highly enlightened, particularly when it was done at the behest of a cultivated heritor or local landholder. At such as Dunfermline, Melrose and Jedburgh, for example, one factor in the decision was an awareness that removal of the modern additions would allow the medieval fabric to be appreciated more fully, and steps were taken to conserve the early work. Elsewhere, however, it appears to have been the cost of maintaining the old fabric, or the need for a more convenient building that led to the move. In some cases, such as Tongland, where it seems that part of the abbey was incorporated in the pre-1813 parish church, this unfortunately means that there is almost nothing left of the abbey church. Probably the last major loss was that of the Observant Franciscan church in Aberdeen which, despite opposition within the university, was demolished to make way for the expansion of Marischal College in 1902.

Despite the scale of the architectural losses we do at least still have a tolerably clear

98 *The abbey of Iona as restored in modern times for the Iona Community.*

idea of the range and quality of buildings produced for the medieval religious houses, particularly since the evidence they provide is supplemented by that afforded by other types of ecclesiastical building. This is less the case for the furnishings and decoration which provided the setting for worship within those churches, where the losses caused by the Reformation have been devastating. We are least unfortunate in the field of stone fixtures – there are still a number of examples of sedilia and piscinas, such as those at Crossraguel, and there are also some splendid tombs and effigies including those at Inchmahome, Dundrennan and Fearn (99). Some fine tile pavements have also been found through excavation, notably at Newbattle (100) and Melrose, and at North Berwick a tile kiln has also been investigated.

The loss of painted work, however, is almost complete, other than the fascinating decoration in the chapter-house of Dryburgh, the painting in a tomb recess at Inchcolm, and some traces of architectural decoration at Torphichen. Similarly, although excavation has provided many fragments of stained glass, the largest single group of fragments is from Holyrood, and we can form no estimate of the prevailing quality of Scottish stained glass from such slight evidence. Moving on to wooden furnishings, apart from some carved timber fragments which may have come from Arbroath and Balmerino, there is very little woodwork indeed; we have to look to Dunblane Cathedral and King's College Aberdeen to appreciate how the carved choir stalls, for example, are likely to have looked. One exceptional survival in the field of monastic furnishings was the brass eagle lectern from Holyrood, which was taken as a trophy of war in 1544 and presented to a church in St Albans.

Assessed on the basis of so few survivors, it might be thought that Scottish monastic churches were only very poorly furnished, but we know this was certainly not the case, since there is abundant documentary evidence of late medieval activity in this field. In the fifteenth century Melrose was so anxious to have choir stalls of the right quality that it arranged to buy them from Bruges, even if it had to go to law before it obtained what had been ordered. We also know of an organ being brought from Flanders for Fearn, of vestments and hangings from Bruges for

99 *The north transept of Dundrennan Abbey church, showing the tomb recess and effigy thought to be of Alan, Lord of Galloway.*

100 *Many monastic churches would have had elaborately-patterned tiled pavements, though few of these now survive. The tiles shown here were found through excavation at Newbattle Abbey.*

Holyrood, of Flemish altarpieces being bought for Pluscarden, and of Flemish vestments at Kinloss. Paisley had an imported altarpiece which it was proudly claimed was the stateliest and most costly in Scotland. All of these were, of course, lost without trace, as were the many pieces produced more locally.

The turning tide of appreciation

Taking account of all of this, it is probably true to say that Scotland's cumulative losses at the Reformation and over the ensuing centuries were proportionately greater than those suffered elsewhere in Europe. However, on a more positive note, procedures for the state to maintain what remained of monastic architecture began to emerge relatively early in Scotland. The crown's assumption of certain ecclesiastical revenues both under the Act of Annexation of 1587, and following the abolition of episcopacy in 1689, meant that, as interest in medieval architecture re-emerged, the state was occasionally prepared to provide funds for its conservation. At St Rule's Church in St Andrews, for example, the Barons of the Exchequer supported work carried out as early as 1789. The impetus for such works increased after Robert Reid became King's Architect in Scotland in 1808, and even more after a separate Scottish Office of Works was briefly set up under his leadership in 1827. He prepared reports on the conservation needs of a number of monastic churches, though it can be rather disconcerting to read in an otherwise judiciously phrased report of 1829 on Dunfermline that it 'does not either in its general features or details exhibit anything very interesting in an architectural point of view'.

By this stage, of course, monastic remains had for some time been favourite themes for romantic contemplation as pleasing ruins within the Scottish landscape. A number of landscape artists were giving eloquent expression to their melancholic beauties, while the novels of Sir Walter Scott were encouraging a wider interest in their history. Scott was, in addition, instrumental in encouraging publication of some of the documentation associated with them. Exceptionally, John Slezer had published detailed engravings of several as early as 1693. But, more recently, Thomas Pennant had published views and descriptions of a number in his volumes of Scottish tours, the first of which had appeared in 1771, while Francis Grose was to publish more in 1789–91. They were evidently becoming essential viewing for the enlightened traveller. Around the same time Captain (later General) George Hutton was beginning his collections of information, with the unfulfilled ambition of publishing an account of monastic remains.

Cultivated appreciation of the remains was therefore being reflected in positive intervention by both private landholders and the state. Although there were to be further losses, religious animosities were by that stage sufficiently cooled for monastic remains to be appreciated on their own terms. One of the great achievements of the nineteenth century was to be the publication of much of the surviving documentation of the monasteries by Cosmo Innes, David Laing, John Stuart and others. Regrettably, however, the dawn of scholarly study of the architectural remains which had been seen in the years around 1800 was not immediately followed up by a bright morning; indeed, it was not to be until the later decades of the century that the first serious studies of Scottish medieval church architecture as a whole were published. Nevertheless, the importance of preserving the remains had been established, and has rarely been challenged since.

The Religious Orders Represented in Scotland

The Benedictine monks (also known as the Black Monks from the colour of their habit). Most monks in the western church can be regarded in one sense as Benedictine, since they nearly all followed the rule which had been compiled by St Benedict of Nursia for his monks at Monte Cassino, at a date after around 525. However, the orders which later emerged were usually differentiated by other names, and it was the monasteries which did not belong to those newer orders which came to be known specifically as Benedictine.

In the earlier centuries of monasticism there had been no attempt to group monasteries into the interlinked networks that were known as orders. Most of the greater monasteries were independent houses under the leadership of an abbot, and were therefore known as abbeys; though there were smaller houses under the leadership of a prior, which were known as priories, and which in some cases might be dependent on an abbey. In the years around 800, in those parts of Europe under the control of the Emperor Charlemagne, many religious houses came to be more strictly organized and interrelated when St Benedict of Aniane became what was almost the chief abbot of the empire. But even then the relationship between monasteries might vary considerably, and most were still essentially independent. There were further attempts to form regional groupings for those monasteries which followed the Benedictine rule, and were not affiliated to any of the newer orders, at the fourth Lateran Council in 1216, but even that had only a certain amount of success.

In Scotland the first Benedictine community was probably that established at Dunfermline (Fife) by St Margaret not long after 1070. There was a later abbey at Iona (Argyll), and priories at Coldingham (Berwickshire), on the Isle of May (Fife) at Urquhart (Moray) and possibly also at Rhynd (Perthshire).

The Cluniac monks. It is almost inevitable in a spiritual movement such as monasticism that high ideals of austerity and self-denial become diluted after a period, and that there is then an attempt to re-establish first principles. (To some extent this is what had already happened with the reforms of St Benedict of Aniane in the later eighth and early ninth centuries, referred to above.) One of the most important early attempts to restore the original purity of monasticism took place in the tenth century, when the abbey of Cluny was founded in Burgundy in 909 by Duke William of Aquitaine. What was achieved there so impressed many church leaders and secular magnates that the community was asked to carry out reforms at other monasteries, and eventually a network of houses was created which owed varying forms of allegiance to the abbot of Cluny. Initially there was no intention of founding an order as such, although this eventually happened, with the abbots or priors of the dependent houses subject to the abbot of Cluny in the same way as a feudal vassal owed allegiance to his lord.

When the influence of the order was at its highest, the abbots of Cluny were among the most powerful men in Europe, and Urban II, one of the great reforming popes of the eleventh century, had himself earlier been a monk of Cluny. The order placed particular stress on the idea that its members should offer to God the very best they could and, as a result, Cluniac houses were often vast and richly decorated groups of buildings, while the services became longer and more complex, with ever more time being spent in church.

In Scotland there were two Cluniac houses, both of which eventually became full abbeys as the original ties with Cluny became weaker. The older was at Paisley (Renfrewshire), which had originally been established at Renfrew in about 1163, and Paisley had a daughter house at Crossraguel (Ayrshire). The small Benedictine priory on the Isle of May may also have been Cluniac in its observances at one stage of its history, though this is uncertain.

The Cistercian monks (also known as the White Monks). The magnificence of the Cluniacs came to be regarded by many as contrary to the spirit of humility and poverty as the basis of monasticism. Around the turn of the eleventh and twelfth centuries, at a time which was perhaps as remarkable for the search for religious renewal as was to be the period of the Reformation in the sixteenth century, a number of fresh attempts to revert to more austere forms of monastic life emerged. The most influential of these was that centred on Cîteaux which, like Cluny, was in Burgundy in eastern France. The order was founded by St Robert of Molesme in 1098, but its great period of influence really began after St Stephen Harding became its third abbot in 1109, and even more after St Bernard joined the order in 1121. By the time of Bernard's death in 1153 the order embraced about five hundred houses.

The order turned its back on the world with the greatest strictness, and practised such extremes of self-denial that life-expectancy for its monks was considerably reduced; it also insisted on sites that were away from centres of population and aimed at architectural simplicity in its buildings. Services were much less elaborate than with the Cluniacs and there was greater emphasis on physical work. Nevertheless, in order to free the monks for spiritual activities, much of the daily work came to be carried out by illiterate *conversi* (lay brethren), who are thus found in greater numbers with the Cistercians than with other orders. Despite the order's rejection of the world, St Bernard became much involved in church affairs and eventually, when the order was at the height of its influence, a pupil of his in 1145 became pope as Eugenius III.

David I introduced the order to Scotland at Melrose (Roxburghshire) in 1136, bringing monks from Rievaulx in Yorkshire. Another daughter house of Rievaulx was established at Dundrennan (Kirkcudbrightshire). Daughter houses of Melrose were founded at Newbattle (Midlothian), Kinloss (Moray), Coupar Angus (Perthshire) and Balmerino (Fife). Kinloss had daughter houses at Culross (Fife) and Deer (Aberdeenshire), while Dundrennan had daughter houses at Glenluce (Wigtonshire) and Sweetheart (Kirkcudbrightshire). The only Cistercian house in Scotland which was not a part of this family tree was Saddell (Argyll), which – as might be expected in western Scotland – was a daughter of Mellifont in Ireland. The family relationships between Cistercian houses were very important and were reinforced by regular General Chapters, which the heads of all houses were expected to attend.

The Tironensian monks (also known as the Grey Monks). Among other attempts to return to the original spirit of the Benedictine rule around this time was one led by another St Bernard. The order took its name from the abbey of Tiron near Chartres, which was founded in 1109. The Tironensians were never to be as popular as the Cistercians and, apart from St Dogmael's in Pembrokeshire, there were only a few small cells or priories in other parts of Britain, several of which were suppressed well before the Reformation.

However, the work of St Bernard of Tiron fired the imagination of David I, whose foundation for the order at Selkirk in 1113 is of particular importance as the first house for any of the reformed orders anywhere in Britain. This house was very soon moved to Kelso (Roxburghshire), and there were other important abbeys at Arbroath (Angus), Kilwinning (Ayrshire) and Lindores (Fife). Smaller priories were founded at Fogo (Roxburghshire), Fyvie (Aberdeenshire) and Lesmahagow (Lanarkshire).

1112 (or 1113)

The Valliscaulian monks. A somewhat later and even less well-known order which was to attract patronage in Scotland was that originating at Val des Choux (valley of the herbs or of the cabbages), near Dijon in France. This order belonged to a further phase of monastic renewal in the early thirteenth century, and its formal institution can be dated to a bull of Innocent III signed in 1205. In many respects the order was a reversion to the primitive spirit of the Cistercians in the time of St Bernard, though it was also influenced by the Carthusians.

There were three Valliscaulian priories in Scotland, all of which were founded within or around the fringes of the Highland area in 1230-1. They were at Ardchattan (Argyll), Beauly (Inverness-shire) and Pluscarden (Moray).

The Carthusian monks. With the Carthusians the spirit of monasticism was combined with the way of life of hermits. The order was founded by St Bruno in 1084 at La Grande Chartreuse, near Grenoble in south-eastern France. The monks spent much of their lives in individual cells grouped around a large cloister, and on weekdays came together in the church for no more than three of the services. On Sundays and a certain number of feast days life was more communal, but even so the individual monks spent much of their time in isolation. Each of their cells was divided into spaces for work, prayer and sleep, and each had a garden and a water supply. Most of the monks' meals were served to them by lay brethren through a hatch which permitted no visual contact. For a Carthusian to survive he had to have a high sense of vocation, and it was the proud boast of the order that they never required to be reformed, because they never lost their original spirit.

Only one Carthusian house was ever founded in Scotland; it was established by James I on the outskirts of Perth in 1429.

The Augustinian canons (also known as the Black Canons). Although it became usual for monks to be ordained as priests, in most orders it was never considered necessary for all members to be priests, and in the earlier days of monasticism the majority were not. However, in the several periods at which there were revivals of the monastic ideal, there was also a parallel tendency for groups of non-monastic clergy to emulate the communally disciplined life of the monks. The origins of such communities of priests – usually known as canons – go back a long way. As early as the eighth century some bodies of priests serving major churches on the Continent had organized themselves on an essentially monastic basis. But in the second half of the eleventh century, following recommendations by the Council of Rome in 1059, there was a new impetus for founding such communities of canons. Many of these came to be known as Augustinian Canons, since they considered they were following the teaching of St Augustine of Hippo, who had died in 430.

The Augustinian Canons had a less rigid constitution than any orders of monks, and tended to be more adaptable to unusual circumstances. Since they were priests, they might also be expected to serve the spiritual needs of the layfolk living in the vicinity of their community, or whose churches had been given to them. Although several Scottish foundations for the order were abbeys on the grandest scale, others were very modest establishments set up within existing churches; significantly, many of these smaller houses were still being founded in the course of the thirteenth and early fourteenth centuries, by which time the orders of monks were no longer attracting much new patronage. The Augustinians were also a particularly convenient order for a founder who wished to supplant an existing body of clerics. Several houses of Culdees, for example, were transformed into Augustinian priories, with the old clergy sometimes being given the option to adapt to new ways or to leave.

The first Scottish house of the order was founded at Scone (Perthshire) by Alexander I in about 1120, and other major houses were established at Cambuskenneth (Stirlingshire), Holyrood (Midlothian), Inchaffray (Perthshire), Inchcolm (Fife), Jedburgh (Roxburghshire) and St Andrews (Fife). Most of these eventually became abbeys. There were smaller priories at Abernethy (Perthshire), Blantyre (Lanarkshire), Canonbie (Dumfriesshire), Inchmahome (Perthshire), Loch Leven (Kinross-shire), Monymusk (Aberdeenshire), Oronsay (Argyll), Pittenweem (Fife), Restenneth (Perthshire), St Mary's Isle (Kirkcudbrightshire) and St Fillan's (Perthshire). Many of these priories were on the sites of earlier foundations.

The Premonstratensian canons (also known as the White Canons). As with the monks, the history of the canons included several attempts to re-establish an even stricter way of life around the later eleventh and earlier twelfth centuries. One of those attempts was made at Arrouaise, where its abbot Gervase (1121-47) copied the rigours of the Cistercian monks. The only Arrouaisian house in Scotland was at Cambuskenneth, and that later became an ordinary member of the Augustinian order. A more influential reform of the Augustinian life was that introduced by St Norbert of Xanten, who founded the abbey of Prémontré in north-eastern France in 1121. Norbert was a close friend of St Bernard, and the life of his canons therefore also tended to develop on similar lines to that of the Cistercians. However, Norbert had originally intended that his canons should be active preachers and evangelists, and it was only after he was succeeded as abbot by Hugh de Fosses in 1125 (when Norbert became archbishop of Magdeburg) that the canons became more fully enclosed on the Cistercian pattern.

The order was probably introduced to Scotland at Dryburgh (Berwickshire) in 1150, with a further abbey being founded at Soulseat (Wigtonshire) soon afterwards, while a priory was attached to the cathedral at Whithorn (Wigtonshire) in about 1175. The other Scottish abbeys for the order were founded in the early thirteenth century, and were at Fearn (Ross), Holywood (Dumfriesshire) and Tongland (Kirkcudbrightshire).

The Trinitarians (sometimes also known as the Red Friars). The Trinitarians, a rather confusing group, were founded shortly before 1200 at Cerfroy in north-eastern France. Despite being often misleadingly described as friars, their way of life was more like that of the Augustinian Canons, although their original function was the ransoming from the Saracens of captured Christians. Initially each house consisted of three priest brethren and three lay brethren under the leadership of a prior.

The earliest of their houses in Scotland was

that at Berwick, which was probably founded around the 1240s. There were also houses at Aberdeen, Dirleton (East Lothian), Dunbar (East Lothian), Fail (Ayrshire), Houston (East Lothian), Peebles and Scotlandwell (Kinross-shire), though some of these were very small and little more than cells dependent on other houses.

Orders of Knights. During the great age of the Crusades, and particularly in the early twelfth century, a number of orders of knights were established who took vows to lead a monastic life. Two of these, the Templars and Hospitallers, were introduced to Scotland by David I. The first house of Knights Templars had been set up in Jerusalem in 1118, and their chief function was to protect pilgrims to the holy shrines. Their way of life was similar to that of the Cistercians. In Scotland they had houses at Temple (Midlothian) and Maryculter (Kincardineshire), but they may have had others elsewhere, including Carnbee (Fife). The order was suppressed in 1312, following accusations of scandalous behaviour, and their possessions were then supposed to have been passed over to the Knights Hospitallers.

The role of the Knights Hospitallers was to provide for the poor and sick and to protect pilgrims on their way to the Holy Land; their way of life was based on that of the Augustinians. The main house of the order in Scotland was at Torphichen (West Lothian), and there could possibly have been another at Kirkliston (West Lothian). In addition, Temple and Maryculter eventually passed from the Templars to the Hospitallers.

The Dominican friars (also known as the Friars Preachers and as the Black Friars). The greatest innovation in the religious life of the thirteenth century was the emergence of the orders of friars. Previous attempts to revert to an essentially apostolic way of life had been hampered by the need to acquire permanent endowments, but the friars aimed to live on the charity of those to whom they ministered. They were thus known as mendicants (beggars). The particular target of their ministry was the population of the cities, where heresy found dangerously fertile ground.

The Dominicans were established in 1215 by St Dominic, at Toulouse in south-western France, where heresy was especially rife. Dominic, a Spanish Augustinian, was a highly practical leader, and organized his order in a way which allowed it to spread rapidly, copying much of the spirit of the Augustinians. As part of the effort to combat heresy the order established links with the new centres of learning which grew into the universities; rather less attractively, it also became closely associated with the Inquisition.

The order was introduced to Scotland by Alexander II in 1230, and in the course of the thirteenth century houses were established at Aberdeen, Ayr, Berwick, Edinburgh, Elgin, Glasgow, Inverness, Montrose (Angus), Perth, Stirling and Wigtown. Later, houses were also founded at Dundee, Haddington (East Lothian), St Andrews (Fife) and St Monans (Fife).

The Franciscan friars (also known as the Friars Minor and as the Grey Friars). The Franciscan Friars emerged at exactly the same date as the Dominicans, and their founder, St Francis of Assisi, was apparently a great influence on St Dominic. The two also received papal approval for their way of life in the same year, 1215. However, whereas the practical Dominic had organized his friars so that it was possible for the order to spread rapidly and effectively, Francis probably never intended to found an order as such. He regarded his fellow friars simply as a loosely-knit group of like-minded souls intent on spreading their message to all who needed it, and otherwise leading a hermit-like life of prayer and self-denial. As a result there was always scope for conflict between those friars who wished absolutely to renounce all worldly possessions, and those who took a more practical view of the need to have bases from which to operate. There was also scope for conflict with members of the church hierarchy, who saw outright rejection of property as a criticism of their own wealth. At an early stage the more extreme wing of the order, known as the Spirituals, was suppressed, but another division later emerged between the established element within the order, known as the Conventuals, and a more fervent group known as the Observants

The first Franciscan house in Scotland was possibly that at Berwick, which appears to date from 1231. Other houses were founded in the thir-

teenth century at Dumfries, Dundee, Haddington, Roxburgh and perhaps also at Inverkeithing (Fife). Houses were later founded at Lanark in the earlier fourteenth century and at Kirkcudbright in the mid-fifteenth century. By that stage, however, the new asceticism of the Observants was becoming more attractive to potential patrons and benefactors than were the older ways of the Conventuals, and the Observants were in fact the only religious group to enjoy significant numbers of new foundations throughout the second half of the fifteenth century. They were introduced to Scotland by Queen Mary of Gueldres, and their Edinburgh house was probably founded in the 1460s. Their other houses were at Aberdeen, Ayr, Elgin, Glasgow, Jedburgh, Perth, St Andrews (Fife) and Stirling.

The Carmelite friars (also known as the White Friars). The Carmelites had their origins in groups of European hermits who had gathered around Mount Carmel in the Holy Land, and who returned to Europe in the train of the Crusaders in the thirteenth century. The earliest house of the order in Scotland was at either Tullilam (Perth) or Berwick. There were eventually also houses at Aberdeen, Banff, Edinburgh, Inverbervie (Kincardineshire), Irvine (Ayrshire), Kingussie (Inverness-shire), Linlithgow (West Lothian), Luffness (East Lothian) and South Queensferry (West Lothian).

Other orders of friars. Among the various other orders of friars, two were represented in Scotland, both having houses at Berwick. The Augustinian Friars, an order established in 1256, had a house there before the end of the thirteenth century. The house of the Friars of the Sack was established in 1267, but had only a very short life, since all such lesser orders of friars were abolished by the Council of Lyons in 1274.

Houses of nuns. Medieval man had a strangely ambivalent attitude towards women. On the one hand they were seen as a source of temptation and a cause of sin, as typified in the person of Eve, while on the other they were idealized because of the role the Virgin had played in bearing the Son of God and thus ensuring the salvation of mankind. Despite the fact that noble women had magnificently led communities both of women alone and of men and women together in Saxon England and Merovingian Gaul, for example, many monastic leaders were distinctly unhappy about encouraging female vocations. This was not least because of the threat they were thought to represent to the moral safety of those who would have to act as their spiritual directors. Nevertheless, many of the orders of monks, canons and friars came to have associated orders of nuns, even though there was no question whatever of the canonesses being in priestly orders, and there could equally clearly be no possibility of any nun pursuing the same mendicant life as a friar. Most of these houses of nuns were relatively small in scale and only modestly endowed.

The Benedictines had a single priory of nuns at Lincluden (Kirkcudbrightshire), which was suppressed in the late fourteenth century. Cistercian nunneries were far more numerous, being founded at Berwick, Coldstream (Berwickshire), Eccles (Berwickshire), Elcho (Perthshire), Haddington (East Lothian), Manuel (Stirlingshire), North Berwick (East Lothian), St Bothan's (Berwick-shire) and St Evoca (Kirkcudbrightshire). The Augustinian canonesses had houses at Iona (Argyll) and Perth. So far as the mendicant orders were concerned the Dominicans were represented at the important Edinburgh priory of Sciennes, while there were Franciscan priories at Aberdour (Fife) and Dundee.

Double houses. There were various attempts throughout the Middle Ages to found mixed houses of both men and women in several parts of Europe. Some of these were highly distinguished establishments although, human nature and susceptibilities being as they are, others were failures. The only double house which may have been planned in medieval Scotland was for Gilbertine nuns and canons at Dalmilling (Ayrshire), and it is doubtful if it ever became fully viable. This order had been founded by St Gilbert of Sempringham in 1131, who held the living of that name in Lincolnshire. The nuns followed the rule of St Benedict, and the canons that of St Augustine, while the lay brethren who served them were organized on Cistercian lines.

Gazetteer of Monastic Sites

This gazetteer gives a brief account of most of the monastic sites of which there are significant upstanding remains. However, it must not be assumed that all of these are accessible to the public, and certainly no attempt should be made to visit any site which is on private land without first obtaining the permission of the owner. Sites which have monastic churches that are still at least partly in use for worship are marked with a cross (+); sites which are monuments in state care, most of which are open on a regular basis, are marked with an asterisk (*). At a time of pending change in local government boundaries it has been felt best to revert to the old county names.

*Abernethy (Perthshire), site of early monastery. There could have been a bishop's church on this site in the early eighth century. However, there is known to have been a community of Culdees and other clergy here around 1100, and the round tower of Irish type may have been built for them, though there appears to be earlier work at the base. An Augustinian priory was founded around the 1270s, but this had been superseded by a college by the mid-fourteenth century, and nothing remains of either.

*Arbroath (Angus), Tironensian abbey. The abbey was founded by King William the Lion in 1178. There are substantial remains of the large church, which was probably started towards the end of that century, including the south transept, the twin-towered west front and the sacristy and treasury block added in the fifteenth century. Little remains of the main conventual buildings,

though the complex plan, with a second courtyard to the south of the cloister, has been excavated. However, the abbot's house, the main gate and a stretch of the precinct wall are particularly impressive.

*Ardchattan (Argyll), Valliscaulian priory. The priory was founded by Duncan McDougall in 1230-1. The main surviving fragments are of the original transepts and the lower walls of the rebuilt choir. Parts of the conventual buildings are embodied in the house to its south, which is still occupied.

Balmerino (Fife), Cistercian abbey. Founded in about 1227 by Ermengarde, widow of William the Lion, and her son Alexander II, it had a characteristic Cistercian plan to the eastern parts of the church, with a single aisle on the south side of the nave. Parts of the south and west walls survive. The cloister was on the north side, and the east range with a fine chapter-house is the best preserved part through having being converted for use as a house after the Reformation.

*Beauly (Inverness-shire), Valliscaulian priory. Founded by John Bisset around 1230. The walls of the church, an elongated aisle-less rectangle with a lateral chapel on each side (but bereft of a second chapel added on the north) survive almost complete. The west front was rebuilt in the sixteenth century.

*Birsay, Brough of (Orkney), possible site of monastery. The rectangular arrangement of buildings to the north of the early twelfth-century church could have belonged to a short-lived monastery, though they could equally have formed an episcopal residence. There may also have been an earlier religious settlement on the site.

Blantyre (Lanarkshire), Augustinian priory. A small house founded around the 1240s by the Earl of Dunbar, its scant remains on the banks of the Clyde are now largely lost within an industrial landscape.

***Brechin** (Angus), site of early monastery. The round tower at the south-west corner of the cathedral is a more lavish version of its counterpart at Abernethy; its finest feature is a richly carved doorway. There was a community here by the 970s, but the tower is unlikely to be before the late eleventh century. There were Culdees serving the bishop into the first half of the thirteenth century, by which time rebuilding of the cathedral was under way.

***Cambuskenneth** (Stirlingshire), Augustinian abbey. It was originally founded in the 1140s for the Arrouaisians by David I, in a loop of the Forth below Stirling Castle; that order was later absorbed by the Augustinians. The foundations of the church are of the later twelfth and early thirteenth centuries. The heavily restored but still complete bell tower to the north is largely of the late thirteenth century. There are scant remains of the east and south claustral ranges, and further remains to the south-east, on the river bank.

+**Coldingham** (Berwickshire), Benedictine priory. The priory originated in the gift of the lands to Durham Cathedral Priory by King Edgar in 1098, and there was some form of monastic presence here by 1139. The best surviving part is the aisle-less rectangular monastic choir, which is now the parish church, and which probably dates from the later twelfth century. The details of the clear-storey arcades on the north and east sides are particularly fine. Fragments of the earlier crossing and of the later south transept also survive. There are remains of claustral ranges south of the choir.

Coupar Angus (Perthshire), Cistercian abbey. A royal foundation of the mid-twelfth century, this became the richest Cistercian house in Scotland. The only upstanding fragment is a gatehouse, but there are many carved and moulded stones around the modern church.

***Crossraguel** (Ayrshire), Cluniac abbey. The lands were granted to Paisley in the early thirteenth century by the heir of the Earl of Carrick, with the intention that a monastery should be founded. This was achieved towards the end of the century. The architectural remains of the abbey are among the most extensive in Scotland. The shell of the basically rectangular church with a polygonal eastern apse still stands, together with parts of the east and south claustral ranges and the remains of an abbatial residence to the south-east of the main complex. There is also an imposing gatehouse into the precinct. The quality of the work in the choir and adjoining sacristy and chapter-house is notably high, and is traditionally associated with Abbot Colin (1460–91).

+***Culross** (Fife), Cistercian abbey. Founded in about 1217 by the Earl of Fife on the site of an earlier community, Culross has the most complete Cistercian church of the so-called 'Bernardine' type (a simple rectangular presbytery flanked by transepts with chapels on their eastern face). The eastern parts of the church – encompassing the presbytery, transepts and monks' choir – remain in use, and are of additional interest since the construction of a fifteenth-century tower embodied the original stone screen at the west end of the monks' choir. There are substantial remains of the west claustral range, and partial remains of the south and east ranges.

***Deer** (Aberdeenshire), Cistercian abbey. The abbey was founded on or near an early monastic site by the Earl of Buchan in 1219. The remains are fragmentary, and extensively reconstructed.

***Dryburgh** (Berwickshire), Premonstratensian abbey. This enchantingly situated abbey was founded in 1150 by Hugh de Moreville, Constable of Scotland. The earliest work is in the east range, including a chapter-house with fine painted decoration. The abbey church was built in the later twelfth and thirteenth centuries, and its most complete elements are the north side of the choir and parts of the transepts. The west end of the nave was rebuilt in the fifteenth century after English attacks. The remains of the refectory include a fine rose window in the west gable.

Dunbar (East Lothian), Trinitarian house. Founded around the 1240s by the Earl of Dunbar and March, only the crossing area – converted into a dovecot – still stands. This is a relic of the type of 'walkway' more usually associated with mendicant houses, in which two walls separate choir and nave and are bridged by arches carrying a slender tower. Excavations in 1981 indicated that both choir and nave were of rectangular plan, and revealed the remains of a fine tiled floor in the former.

*Dundrennan** (Kirkcudbrightshire), Cistercian abbey. This abbey was founded in 1142 by Fergus lord (or king) of Galloway with the support of David I. The beautiful east walls of the transepts stand to full height, and are important for the light they cast on the role of the Cistercians in introducing early Gothic architecture to Scotland in the later twelfth century. Of the monastic buildings the most delightful is the entrance to the chapter-house, rebuilt in the early thirteenth century.

*Dunfermline** (Fife), Benedictine abbey. Established as Scotland's first Benedictine community by St Margaret not long after 1070, it was re-founded as a major abbey by David I in 1128. It was the burial place of several generations of monarchs, and was planned on a magnificent scale. The nave of the twelfth century church stands complete, though its western towers were rebuilt in the fifteenth, sixteenth and nineteenth centuries. There is an early nineteenth-century church on the site of the choir, at the east end of which is a fragment of the mid-thirteenth-century shrine chapel of St Margaret. Apart from the church the finest remains are of the refectory and the guest house. The former, elevated on two storeys of undercroft, was under construction in 1329 with the assistance of Robert I (the Bruce). The guest house may also have been started around the same date, but was remodelled as part of a royal palace for Queen Anne of Denmark in the late sixteenth century.

Eccles (Berwickshire), Cistercian nunnery. The priory was founded in the mid-twelfth century by the Earl of Dunbar, possibly together with David I. There are slight remains of it at the edge of the parish churchyard.

*Eileach-an-Naoimh** (Argyll), site of early monastery. There are substantial structural remains which can presumably be associated with an early community, including cells of beehive shape similar to examples found in Ireland. It has been suggested these were built for a monastery founded by St Brendan, who died in 577, though there can be no certainty of this.

Elcho (Perthshire), Cistercian nunnery. This priory, on the bank of the Tay to the south-east of Perth, was founded before his death in 1241 by David Lindsay. Remains of a basically rectangular church have been exposed by excavation.

+Elgin** (Moray), Franciscan friary. An Observant house, Elgin was probably founded towards the end of the fifteenth century. Its rectangular church stands complete as a result of restoration carried out in 1896 by the architect John Kinross, on behalf of the Marquess of Bute. It now serves the adjacent convent of the Sisters of Mercy.

*Eynhallow** (Orkney), possible site of monastery. There may have been a monastery here in the twelfth century, but none of the buildings to the west and south of the remains of the church are now thought to have belonged to that foundation.

+Fearn** (Ross-shire), Premonstratensian abbey. Probably founded by the Earl of Ross in the 1220s, the abbey church is said to have been rebuilt between 1338 and 1372. This basically rectangular church, partly truncated at its western end, remains in use as the parish church.

*Glenluce** (Wigtonshire), Cistercian abbey. Founded by the Lord of Galloway in the early 1190s, the church was laid out on the usual type of Cistercian plan. Of the monastic buildings the most complete part is the late fifteenth- or early sixteenth-century square chapter-house, which is still vaulted, and there are reconstructed sections of the cloister arcade.

Holyrood (Edinburgh), Augustinian abbey. A foundation of David I dating from 1128, this abbey had a similar relationship to Edinburgh Castle as did Cambuskenneth to Stirling Castle. Of the first church only a door into the cloister survives, the rest of the church having been rebuilt on a grand scale from the later twelfth century onwards. Of this fully vaulted church, only the mainly thirteenth-century nave survived English attacks of the 1540s and the aftermath of the Reformation, and much of that collapsed in the eighteenth century. The chapter-house was a polygonal structure. The palace probably grew up around the core of the medieval royal lodging.

Inchaffray (Perthshire), Augustinian abbey. Occupying the site of an early foundation, it was re-founded for Augustinians by the Earl of Strathearn in 1200. The main upstanding fragment is part of the west range, which was probably adapted as a residence for the commendators shortly before the Reformation.

*****Inchcolm** (Fife), Augustinian priory. The much-rebuilt hermit's cell on this lovely island site may perpetuate that of the hermit who gave Alexander I shelter in 1123. His intention to found a monastery was eventually carried out by David I before his death in 1153. Parts of the church then built still survive, though it was greatly extended in the thirteenth century before being completely replaced by a new church to its east in the early fifteenth century. The fully-vaulted monastic buildings are the most complete in Scotland, but are unusual in several respects. The earliest part is the thirteenth-century polygonal chapter-house. The three cloister walks, occupying the full ground floor of the ranges around the cloister, and surmounted by dormitory, refectory and guest hall, are probably fifteenth century.

*****Inchmahome** (Perthshire), Augustinian priory. Founded in about 1238 by the Earl of Menteith, at an existing church site, this beautifully-sited island monastery was never a large establishment. The church has a single aisle flanking the nave, on the side away from the cloister. The chapter-

house is well-preserved because it was later used as a mausoleum, and now houses some fine effigies.

Inverkeithing (Fife), Franciscan friary. Of the Conventual friary founded around the 1260s the best-preserved portion is the restored guest house, now used as a museum.

Iona (Argyll), site of early monastery. This, the most seminally important early monastery in Scotland, was founded by St Columba in 563 or 565. The most impressive remains are of the earthwork vallum, defining the roughly rectangular precinct. Evidence for the continuing vitality of the community is seen in the magnificent high crosses.

+Iona, Benedictine abbey. Set within the earlier precinct, the medieval abbey was founded by Reginald son of Somerled, lord of the Isles, at a date before 1203. The church and abbey are complete but heavily restored or rebuilt. The earliest part of the cruciform church is the north transept. Apart from the excavated remains of a massive asymmetrical south transept, the rest of the structure dates chiefly from late medieval rebuilding.

Iona, Augustinian nunnery. This most extensive relic of a Scottish nunnery, had the same founder as the nearby abbey. The north arcade and clear-storey, the north chapel, and the west gable of the church stand virtually complete. There are also substantial remains of the refectory.

*****Jedburgh** (Roxburghshire), Augustinian Abbey. Founded in about 1138 by David I and his erstwhile tutor, Bishop John of Glasgow, the magnificent remains of this abbey still represent one of the most impressive sights to face those entering Scotland from the south. The earliest parts are in the western bays of the choir and transepts, but the most complete part is the late twelfth-century nave, the central space of which still stands to full height. South of the church are the fascinating excavated remains of the monastic buildings, rising from the north bank of the Jed Water.

Jedburgh, Franciscan friary. This house of Observants was probably founded in the early sixteenth century. The excavated remains of its conventual buildings represent the most complete plan of any mendicant house so far recovered in Scotland.

*Kelso (Roxburghshire), Tironensian abbey. Moved from Selkirk in 1128, the church then built, with its double-cross plan, was perhaps the most extraordinary Romanesque building in Scotland. Parts of the western transept and tower, and the south-west corner of the nave still stand to full height. Evidence of the main south transept and the infirmary have been found through excavation.

*Kilwinning (Ayrshire), Tironensian abbey. This abbey was probably founded by Richard de Moreville before his death in 1189. The most impressive remains are of the south transept, but there are also fragments of a twin-towered west front of unusual form. The late medieval 'Romanesque revival' entrance front of the chapter-house stands virtually complete.

*Kingarth (Bute), site of early monastery. The settlement is said to have been founded by St Blane in the later sixth century, and there are references to continuing activity in the seventh and eighth centuries. Within the main enclosure was a smaller cemetery, and there are also traces of what appear to have been cells. The main feature of the site is a small mid-twelfth-century church.

Kinloss (Moray), Cistercian abbey. Founded by David I in about 1150, this is one of only two of the order's Scottish churches known to have deviated from the plan particularly associated with the Cistercians. The main upstanding remains are of the south transept and adjacent parlour or sacristy. There are also remains of the abbot's house built for Robert Reid.

+Kirkcudbright, Franciscan friary. A fragment of this Conventual Franciscan house, founded around 1450 by James II, may survive in the modern Episcopalian church.

*Lincluden (Kirkudbrightshire), Benedictine nunnery. Probably founded by Uchtred, son of Fergus lord of Galloway before his death in 1174, it was suppressed at the request of the third Earl of Douglas in 1389 in advance of the foundation of a college. Fragments of the nunnery may survive within the later collegiate buildings.

Lindores (Fife), Tironensian abbey. This house was founded in about 1190 by David Earl of Huntingdon. There are overgrown remains of the presbytery and transepts of the church, of the east conventual range and of the freestanding north-western bell tower. Fragments of a number of outbuildings are also to be seen.

Linlithgow (West Lothian), Carmelite friary. This house was founded in about 1401 by Sir James Douglas of Dalkeith. The church and parts of the conventual buildings were revealed through excavation in 1983–4.

*Loch Leven (Kinross-shire), Augustinian priory (although this site is in the care of the state, it is on an island nature reserve and not normally open to the public). There had been an early community on this island site, and it was re-established for the Augustinians by David I around 1150. The only upstanding fragment is the tiny twelfth-century nave, though there are enigmatic bumps in the ground which may indicate the site of the monastic buildings.

Luffness (East Lothian), Carmelite friary. In existence by 1293, the lower walls of the small rectangular church – divided into two parts by a stone screen – are all that is visible.

Manuel (West Lothian), Cistercian nunnery. This nunnery was founded by Malcolm IV before 1164. Part of its handsome thirteenth-century west gable survives in the slightly surreal setting of a sewage treatment plant.

Mauchline (Ayrshire), Cistercian grange. The tower-house residence of the abbots still stands complete on this grange of the abbey of Melrose. It was built by Abbot Hunter (c.1444–71).

May (Fife), Benedictine priory. A foundation of David I, one range of the conventual buildings on this island site was converted to a residence in the sixteenth century. Recent excavations have located the rectangular church and extended our knowledge of the layout of the site.

*Melrose (Roxburghshire), Cistercian abbey. Perhaps the most beautiful of all Scottish monastic ruins, this was David I's first foundation for the Cistercians, in about 1136. Rebuilding of the church was started after an English attack in 1385, but was never completed; intriguingly, it was laid out to the same basic plan as the original church, albeit on a larger scale. The church is one of the most important indicators of changing architectural attitudes in the later Middle Ages. The main nucleus of monastic buildings has been revealed through excavation, and the commendator's house has been disentangled from later buildings and restored.

+Monymusk (Aberdeenshire), Augustinian priory. There were Culdees here in the twelfth century, who were transformed into Augustinians by around 1245. The basically twelfth-century church remains in use, but almost nothing is known of the conventual buildings.

Newbattle (Midlothian), Cistercian abbey. A foundation of David I and his son Henry Earl of Northumberland in 1140. The church and monastic buildings were excavated for the Marquess of Lothian in the 1870s and 1890s, and are now partly expressed as flower beds. The vaulted undercroft of the east range is still embodied in restored form within the post-Reformation house (now a college). Along with Kinloss this is the only Scottish Cistercian church known not to have been of the so-called 'Bernardine' plan-type.

North Berwick (East Lothian), Cistercian nunnery. Founded by the Earl of Fife around 1150, this was one of Scotland's wealthier nunneries. A range within a ruined later residence may survive from the conventual buildings. An important tile kiln was excavated here in 1927–8.

North Rona (Ross), site of early monastery. The seventh-century St Ronan is said to have lived on this remotest of island sites as a hermit, having been taken there from Lewis by a whale. The rectangular chapel, with corbelled roof construction, was later extended by a second chamber.

Oronsay (Argyll), Augustinian priory. This house was probably founded on the site of an earlier religious settlement by the Lord of the Isles, before the mid-fourteenth century. There are substantial remains of the church and monastic buildings. Particularly fascinating are the partly rebuilt triangular-headed cloister arcades, with stones set against each other in house-of-cards fashion.

+Paisley (Renfrewshire), Cluniac abbey. The foremost Scottish Cluniac abbey was founded by Walter, Steward of Scotland, in the 1160s. The impressive nave incorporates work of the thirteenth, fourteenth and fifteenth centuries; the transepts are heavily restored, and the extraordinarily long choir is a modern reconstruction. Fragments of the monastic buildings are incorporated in the adjacent Place of Paisley.

*Peebles, Trinitarian house. Founded towards the end of the thirteenth century in a church said to have housed relics of the true cross, the chief surviving parts are a habitable west tower and the nave. There are also excavated foundations of the conventual buildings.

+Pittenweem (Fife), Augustinian priory. By an only partly understood process of transformation, this became the home of the Benedictine community transferred from the Isle of May by about 1200. The community used an existing church, and their domestic buildings were around a detached courtyard to its south. Most of the courtyard buildings have been remodelled since the Reformation, including the gate into the precinct.

+Pluscarden (Moray), Valliscaulian priory. Founded in 1230 by Alexander II, this was architecturally the most ambitious house of the order. The elegant choir and transepts of the thirteenth-century church, together with the east conventual range, survive virtually complete, albeit extensively remodelled in the late Middle Ages – by when the abbey had become Benedictine – and more recently. They now house a Benedictine community.

*Restenneth (Angus), Augustinian priory. The idea that this was where King Nechtan built a church with masons sent from Northumberland in 710 is now generally rejected. Nevertheless, the base of the tower appears to be at least as early as the eleventh century. The priory may have been founded by David I in the second quarter of the twelfth century, as a daughter house of Jedburgh, and the upper parts of the tower are probably of that date. The aisle-less choir and nave to either side of that tower are thirteenth century, as may be parts of the monastic buildings.

Saddell (Argyll), Cistercian abbey. Founded by Reginald, Lord of the Isles before 1207, there are only scant remains of the simple cruciform church and the south range. It had been suppressed by about 1507.

*St Andrews (Fife), Augustinian cathedral priory. From at least the ninth century this site had become the administrative centre of the Scottish church, and large numbers of carved stones survive from the earlier part of that century onwards, giving evidence of its creativity. The Augustinian priory, first mooted in the 1120s and finally established in the 1140s, initially used St Rule's church, before the new cathedral – the largest in Scotland – was started around 1160. It was consecrated in 1318. The monastic buildings of various dates, and partly reconstructed by the Marquess of Bute in the late nineteenth century, are around a large cloister to the south of the cathedral. The prior, who was eventually allowed to wear the mitre (one of the symbols of episcopal status) took precedence over all other Scottish heads of religious houses, including abbots.

*St Andrews, Dominican friary. This house was in existence by 1464, but was revived in the early sixteenth century and rebuilt with money left by Bishop Elphinstone of Aberdeen in 1514. The only surviving part is a polygonal lateral chapel which projected from the north flank of the church.

St Fillan's (Perthshire), Augustinian priory. A small house which grew from a gift of Robert I in 1317, the only upstanding remains are confusing fragments of what was probably a simple church.

+St Monan's (Fife), Dominican friary. The Dominicans were installed here by James III in 1471, within a chapel that had been first built by David II a century earlier. That chapel was partly remodelled, but it seems it was never served by more than two friars. The building, which is now T-shaped with a squat spired tower, is most attractively sited on the sea-shore.

Scone (Perthshire), Augustinian abbey. This was Scotland's first Augustinian house, having been founded by Alexander I in about 1120, on what may have been a site occupied by an earlier community. Little more than a few scattered carved and moulded fragments serving as garden ornaments are now to be seen. The stone of Scone, on which Scottish kings were seated at their inauguration, was kept in the abbey until removed to Westminster Abbey by Edward I in 1296.

Sgòr Nam Ban-Naomha (Argyll), site of early monastery. The remains probably reflect two main campaigns. The first phase included the kidney-shaped enclosure wall and a number of buildings within it, including what may have been a bath-house. Several hut circles were added later, both within and outside the main enclosure. The whole complex has an unexpectedly sophisticated water supply for so early a date.

+South Queensferry (West Lothian), Carmelite friary. Founded around 1440 by James Dundas, this church is a remarkably complete survival. The nave was lost in the nineteenth century, but the choir, south transept and central tower were restored for Episcopalian worship in 1889.

*Sweetheart (Kirkcudbrightshire), Cistercian abbey. The last foundation for the Cistercian order in Scotland was endowed by Dervorguilla Balliol in 1273. Its imposing church is a remarkable combination of conservative Cistercian planning together with the most recent architectural detailing, and is one of the first Scottish churches to have been provided with bar tracery. There are remains of the conventual buildings and of the precinct walls.

Tongland (Kirkcudbrightshire), Premonstratensian abbey. Founded by the Lord of Galloway in 1218, only a tiny fragment of the church remains, and that in a rather parlous state.

+*Torphichen** (West Lothian), preceptory of Knights Hospitallers. This was the main house of the Hospitallers in Scotland, and was founded by David I around the mid-twelfth century. The vaulted transepts and tower of the church as rebuilt in the mid-fifteenth century still stand complete. The nave has been rebuilt for the parish church and little recognizably medieval work survives; the choir is almost completely destroyed.

*Whithorn** (Wigtonshire), Premonstratensian cathedral priory. This highly important site is associated with the Celtic and Northumbrian monasteries which developed in the area probably previously occupied by the episcopal centre established by St Ninian in the early fifth century. Something is known of the earlier buildings from excavations, and there are also important early carved stones, but the upstanding structures belong to the medieval cathedral church which was served by a community of Premonstratensian Canons established around the 1170s. Parts of the aisle-less nave were adapted for post-Reformation worship and still stand largely complete. There are also heavily restored undercrofts at the east end of the choir. The modern church stands on the site of the east conventual range.

Further Reading

Monastic history (in general)

Christopher Brooke, *The monastic world*, London, 1974.

C.H. Lawrence, *Medieval monasticism*, London, 1984.

David Knowles, *The monastic order in England*, Cambridge, 2nd ed. 1963.

Monastic buildings

Wolfgang Braunfels, *Monasteries of western Europe*, London, 1972.

Lionel Butler and Chris Given-Wilson, *Medieval monasteries of Great Britain*, London, 1979.

Glyn Coppack, *English Heritage book of abbeys and priories*, London, 1990.

R. Gilyard-Beer, *Abbeys*, London, 1958.

Christopher Norton and David Park, *Cistercian art and architecture in the British Isles*, Cambridge, 1986.

Scottish monastic history within its broader context

G.W.S. Barrow, *The kingdom of the Scots*, London, 1973.

William Moir Bryce, *The Scottish Greyfriars*, 2 vols, Edinburgh, 1909.

Ian B. Cowan and David Easson, *Medieval religious houses, Scotland*, London, 2nd ed. 1976.

Ian B. Cowan, *The Scottish Reformation*, London, 1982.

A.A.M. Duncan, *Scotland, the making of the kingdom*, Edinburgh, 1975.

Charles Thomas, *The Early Christian archaeology of North Britain*, Oxford, 1971.

Scottish monastic buildings

Several of the greater Scottish monasteries are in the care of Historic Scotland, and guide books are available for many of them. Descriptions of a number of religious houses are also to be found in the county inventories of the Royal Commission on the Ancient and Historical Monuments of Scotland.

Although much of the information it contains has inevitably been superseded, the fullest survey of the religious architecture of the Middle Ages is still:

David MacGibbon and Thomas Ross, *The ecclesiastical architecture of Scotland*, 3 vols, Edinburgh, 1896–7.

Useful descriptions of some of the buildings will also be found in:

Stewart Cruden, *Scottish medieval churches*, Edinburgh, 1986.

Index

(Page numbers in **bold** indicate illustrations)

144